SOCIAL PSYCHOLOGY

A GUIDE TO SOCIAL AND CULTURAL PSYCHOLOGY

CONNOR WHITELEY

Any questions about the book, rights licensing, or to contact the author, please email connorwhiteley@connorwhiteley.net

ACKNOWLEDGMENTS

Thank you to my readers without you, I couldn't do what I love.

INTRODUCTION

Whenever people think about psychology, they don't think about biological psychology, cognitive psychology or any other subfields of psychology.

Chances are people think of social psychology and how social groups and processes impact human behaviour.

Whilst, a lot of people who aren't in psychology spit on social psychology for being unscientific and trying to boil down the complexity of social groups and processes into a science is silly.

Personally, I gave those people a kind smile and when they have left I laugh at them.

As a result, social psychology might not have the hard biological facts biological psychology has, but social psychology still has some great experiments that has allowed psychology to discover great and interesting things about how social processes affect us.

From social groups to persuasion to social influence to culture, social psychology covers a lot of ground.

Personally, I think this area of psychology is one of the most interesting because we can apply social psychology to everyday life.

Who is this Book For?

If you're a University student or someone interested in social psychology, and you want a book that breaks content into interesting and easy to understand pieces of information. Then this is the book for you.

I won't give you long boring complex paragraphs filled with head-spinning information.

Instead, I'll give you lots of engaging information and I'll explain how this relates to everyday life.

In other words, this is the sort of textbook I would like for my degree. Engaging without compromising on the content.

Who Am I?

I always like to know who writes whatever nonfiction book I read. So, in case you're like me I'm Connor Whiteley I'm an author of over 30 books and 11 of these are psychology books. Ranging in topics on biological psychology to Forensic Psychology to Clinical Psychology.

Also, I'm a university student at the University of Kent and I'm the host of the weekly The Psychology World Podcast where I talk about psychology news and a range of psychology topics.

Finally, I've interviewed New York Times and USA Today bestselling author J. F Penn as well.

So let's move onto talk about the great topic of social psychology!

PART ONE: INTRODUCTION TO SOCIAL PSYCHOLOGY

CHAPTER 1: HISTORY OF SOCIAL PSYCHOLOGY

Welcome to the start of your social psychology journey.

Personally, I love social psychology but before we dive into the social-psychological topics we need to look at the history of social psychology.

Social psychology started in the 1700s when British scholars started to discuss emotions and interactions, as well as when German scholars and French scholars discussed the self and relationships. These scholars argued that these can be studied as a science as well.

Subsequently, in the 19th-century German scholars referred to the 'collective mind' and Wundt argued that the individual consciousness was influenced by interactions and morality.

Influences on social psychology:

Social psychology isn't its own unique field because it has drawn on multiple influences from a lot of different psychological fields.

Some of these fields include:

- Behaviourism- this focuses only on the behaviour output. This subfield couldn't care less about the internal cognitive structures in the human mind.

Social psychology draws on behaviourism because its behaviourism that gave us information on conditioning and this can potentially apply to multiple social processes.

- Gestalt psychology- this area looks at the whole picture and the needs and desires that influence you, not just reward and punishment.

A key fact about social psychology and psychology in general is that everything influences you even at a basic level.

Historical Context:

Most of the interest from social psychology arouse from historical contexts like the social background of scholars, abuse, world war 2, social and political events. Like Brexit and Darwinian theory (evolution).

All these contexts helped to motivate and provide interest for social psychologists to explore.

CHAPTER 2: HOW DO YOU DO SOCIAL PSYCHOLOGY?

In this chapter, we'll be investigating how social psychology is researched.

In social psychology, you can take two approaches to research.

Firstly, you can take the root of observations. This is where you observe behaviour in order to learn about it.

Secondly, you can take the empirical approach. This is where you take scientific methods and use them to examine behaviour.

Research Process:

The first step to any good piece of social psychological research is to have a good research process.

The research process goes in the following way:

- You create your question. Like: what causes conformity?
- You develop a theory or refer to past theories to answer your question.
- You develop an experiment and then you test your theory.
- If your theory isn't supported then this leads to reduced confidence in theory so you can reject the theory or modify the theory taking you back to the developing experiment phrase.
- If your theory is supported then your confidence in the theory increases.

Overall, the stages of the research process are one big circular cycle as you try to answer your research question.

Tools of Social Psychology:

In social psychology, there is a wide range of research tools that social psychologists can use to study behaviour.

Qualitative:

In short, qualitative research is when you create thick rich descriptions of text as your data instead of hard numbers.

Please see Research in Psychology for more

information.

Some examples of qualitative research methods in social psychology include:

- Thematic analysis- you analyse the themes of a situation to find something.
- Conversational analysis- you analyse the conversation to find something.
- Narrative analysis- one way of doing this type of analysis is by analysing the patient's narratives to discover the patient's emotional state, unconscious thoughts and as a type of therapy.
- Discourse analysis- you analyse any discourse; written, spoken and more; to find something.
- Interpretative phenomenological analysis (IPA)

Quantitative:

The opposite of Qualitative research is quantitative research, where you use hard factual numbers in your research data.

Some examples of this type of research include:

- Surveys and questionnaires
- Experiments
- Field experiments
- Archival experiments
- Observations

- Case study

Issues in Social Psychology:

In this last section, we'll be looking at the many problems that social psychology has faced.

Firstly, social psychology and pretty much all social science fields are prone to sample bias because most psychology participants are from the western world and undergraduate psychology students. Meaning that you potentially cannot say the behaviour showed with these studies are universal as psychology undergraduates are a very small percentage of the human population.

In addition, in reason years social psychology has faced The Crisis where multiple famous research papers that have revolutionised the field and the world were found out to be falsified by the researchers.

Overall, these are only a small number of problems that social psychology faces but it must be remembered that it is only a very select few researchers that falsified data.

CHAPTER 3: WHAT DO GROUPS DO FOR INDIVIDUALS?

Throughout the book, you're going to see a lot about social groups and their negative side from social influence to intergroup relationships. You're going to see quite a bit of negativity surrounding social groups.

So, in this chapter, I wanted to stress that social groups can benefit us a lot.

Interdependence:

Firstly, being a part of a social group gives us more interdependence and people can often achieve more in groups than alone. (Thibaut & Kelley, 1959)

I certainly know this from doing group projects at university because depending on the members of the group. A presentation or report can take half the time.

A classic example of this idea is trade unions (Veenstra & Haslas, 2000) because people who identify highly with the union are more willing to take part in conflicts compared to if they were alone.

Even people with low identification with groups are willing to take part in the action when it's in their own interest.

I did this in 2020 when Audible was (and still is as of January 2021) abusing authors by hiding return data and encouraging customers to read an entire audiobook that they loved and return it.

Yes, it's great for the customers but authors are losing a lot of money to this 'great' benefit to customers.

Therefore, as I'm a member of the Alliance of Independent Authors and I identify highly with the group. I took action by signing some petition, cancelling my audible membership and telling people about the conflict.

Affiliation, similarity, and Support:

Another great benefit of being a part of a social group is grouping together with people who have the same attitudes. (Bairister & Leary, 1995) and the same problems.

This is a great benefit because it allows people to

come together and talk about their attitudes. When it might not be a good thing to talk about their attitudes with other people.

For example, I would talk about my dislike for Brexit with my family and friends, but I wouldn't talk about that topic to a lot of other people.

Furthermore, social groups allow people to feel understood, less alone, and befriended. This can be seen in people that are sad since they seek support. (Gray, Ishii & Ambady, 2011)

Terror Management:

I Think This Benefit Has Definitely Been Proved By The COVID-19 Pandemic Because Let's Face It We Are All Going To Die.

Therefore, People Look For Structure To Confront The Inevitability Of Death. (Greenberg Et Al, 1986)

This Is Provided by group norms, identifiers, values and human company. Also known as social groups.

Need for Social Identity:

We'll discuss social identity a lot more in a few chapters time but social groups are great at providing us with social identity.

This is very important for reducing subjective uncertainty about the world. (Hoggs et al, 2008)

Optimal Distinctness:

Let's face it people love to be special and people want to be different and unique. This is where optimal distinctness comes in because people need to distinguish themselves (Brewer, 1991) but we need to affiliate with others as well.

Therefore, being a part of a group means we get to affiliate with others, but we get to be distinct members of that group and wider society as a whole.

Strategies for Optimal Distinctiveness:

There are a lot of ways to achieve optimal distinctiveness. For example, people can identify with a subgroup of a mainstream group. This allows us to be distinctive and socialize with other people. (Hornsey & Jetten, 2004)

Another strategy is to identify with a non-mainstream group and this is where my strategy comes in. As I'm an author and authors are hardly mainstream, so I get to socialise with other authors. Yet I'm distinctive in terms of I write books and I run my own creative global empire/ business.

You might have your own idea about this strategy. For example, if you're in the UK then during your university years you might have belonged to a non-mainstream society. (club)

I remember one of my friends belonging to the Quidditch society, and yes that is the sport from Harry Potter.

Finally, people can achieve optimal distinctiveness by making themselves unique with a distinct role.

So, you might be the leader of the social group or you might make yourself important in the group. Like: in my university's baking society I'm treasurer in 2020-2021.

Other Benefits of Social Groups Are:

- Positive consequences for the self
- They give us the motivation to protect the group

CHAPTER 4: THE SOCIAL CURE HYPOTHESIS

Following on from the last chapter, the last main benefit of social groups is the Social Cure Hypothesis. This is the idea that our group memberships can help our ability to deal with stress.

Additionally, this is thought to work in two different ways.

Firstly, you have the social route where social groups provide people with the perception of social support and the expectation of helping ingroup memberships. This leads to the ingroup members helping each other and this is especially true when the group is apart of a social network.

Another way how the social cure hypothesis works is by the cognitive route. This is related to how people feel in relation to the social group and the positivity the social group gives people.

For example, the social group gives people Self-continuity when things change for them and their groups provide a stable identity for them.

Finally, the social groups provide people with self-esteem and sometimes people can feel better for being associated with it.

I know this is true for me when I'm having problems at university. I know I'm a part of a large group of students and they can help me.

The Social Cure in Medicine

Sometimes I feel like psychology can be a bit abstract and it doesn't always reflect the real world. So I want to explain how the social cure can be used in the real world.

After trauma and life events, some people have fewer group memberships. This can be used to negatively predict well-being over time.

Therefore, if you use the social cure hypothesis, we know social groups can help with mental health and trauma.

Resulting in psychology being able to counteract this decreased mental health by helping the person to join new groups.

CHAPTER 5: THE SELF AND SELF-AWARENESS

This was the topic that I learned about at university after the boring introduction lectures and I have to say that it was very interesting. I hope you enjoy it as well.

Who are we?

Who are you?

These are great questions that are related to the self.

The self is constantly refined because we are constantly refining ourselves.

Personally, I went through a massive refine in March 2019 as I decided to define myself as an author.

In addition, the Self is intrinsically social and the

self influences our behaviour.

Interestingly, we tend to view our self-relationships with ourselves like they aren't apart of us. Meaning we view them like an outsider, as well as people can have symbolic relationships with themselves. This is where you view our self-relationships as other people interact with us.

I know that that was extremely complex but imagine as if you're in a room, with yourself as your full being then you see another version of yourself may be sitting on the floor. This another version of you is a version of yourself. This version may be your sad self or lonely self.

I know it's very hard, but it will become clearer as you read on.

Finally, it is very important that we control our behaviour and maintain the self that we want others to see.

Self-Schemas:

As previously mentioned, the Self is made up of different dimensions and can be thought as versions and these dimensions are called schemas.

Schemas are a mental framework that influences how we encode, store and retrieve information.

For more information on schemas, please see

Cognitive Psychology.

Furthermore, some schemas are more important than others and you can think of these schemas as parts or dimensions of yourselves. For example, being an author and a psychology student is more important to me than my cooking side.

Therefore, self-schematics are the important parts of the self. Whereas the self aschematic are the less important parts.

Self- Concept and Knowledge:

Whilst these schemas can be about the desired self and undesired self. It must be pointed out that schemas can become all-consuming as the self does influence our daily life.

Meaning if a person has a self-schema about weight. This can lead to excessive weight monitoring.

Self-awareness:

Self-awareness is the psychological state of being aware of your own characteristics, feelings and behaviours. This happens around the age of 18 months.

Public Self-Awareness:

This type of self-awareness is when you have an awareness of the public aspects of yourself, so what other people can see.

This leads to adherence to social norms and society's standards.

However, public self-awareness can be debilitating because of public self-consciousness. This is chronic public self-awareness where a person is too concerned with how they are perceived and evaluated by others.

Private Self-Awareness:

Private self-awareness is an awareness of the private aspect of the self. This can be positive if people focus on positive parts of themselves, but it can be negative, and it can lead to depression if you focus on negative parts of the self.

In my opinion, I am a positive person because I focus on the positive aspects of myself whilst acknowledging the bad as well. For example, I focus on the fact I'm a good psychology student but I'm not the best.

Interestingly, the more self-awareness a person has the more moral and the strong a person adheres to their own attitudes in general.

The Biological Basis of The Self:

Biologically speaking the self is considered to be created in the anterior cingulate cortex. This is responsible for controlling and monitoring your intention behaviour.

This is because this brain area activates when people become self-aware.

CHAPTER 6: THEORIES OF THE SELF

In social psychology, many theories have been created to explain the self.

Multiple Role Theory:

This recognizes that the self is a very complex thing and it proposes that having multiple selves are important.

It's important because it is a benefit to health and wellbeing to have multiple self-identities. This makes you open to new experiences.

In addition, the theory focuses on both the quality of selves and the quantity.

In my opinion, I think this is a good theory because I know from personal experiences that in order to recover when one of your identities or selves is taken apart from you. You need to have other selves to recover.

For example, when something happened to me

that made me have to quit scouting. I had to rely on my other selves and refine myself in order to recover. As beforehand my scouting self was a massive part of my overall self, but as I had my author self and a few other selves. I managed to recover. Meaning that my author self replaced the massive hole that my scouting self left behind.

Overall, I hope that that showed you the importance and benefits of having multiple selves.

<u>Self-Perception Theory:</u>

In this theory, Bem, (1967, 1972) argued that people learn about the self by looking at the behaviour that they do as well as by examining their own thoughts, feelings and behaviours.

In my opinion, this is another good theory because I think that we do learn a lot from examining ourselves as we learn what we think and feel about other topics.

On the other hand, later in this book, I will discuss how people aren't as good as they think they are at knowing what they actually think about something.

<u>Self-Discrepancy Theory:</u>

Our next theory is by Higgins (1987) and it focuses on people's attitudes discrepancies between the actual self and the perceived self. These discrepancies can lead to sadness, disappointment and frustration.

Hence, the need for self-regulation as we attempt to match these desired behaviours.

Within this theory, they are serval, unique terms that are used to describe the self.

- The actual self- how people perceive the self at a given time.
- The ideal self- how the person would like to perceive themselves.
- The ought self- what the person thinks the self ought to be.

Let's use a personal example of these ideas:

- The actual self- I am a good psychology student that is getting good grades.
- The ideal self and the Ought Self- I want to be a great student that is getting great grades.

As I showed you in the example above sometimes the ideal self and the Ought Self can be the same thing.

Subsequently, if there are discrepancies between

the selves then this can lead to different emotional reactions.

Regulatory Focus Theory:

This theory is another theory created by Higgins (1997, 1998) that built upon the self-discrepancy theory to propose people can take two self-regulatory approaches.

The first approach is promotion where people focus on gaining and seeing the ideal self as important. Whereas in the second approach; prevention; people focus on avoiding and preventing as a way to construct the self.

One study on these approaches was a meta-analysis by Bass et al (2008) that found that people with the promotion approach tend to be associated with more creativity.

While the approaches can be changed, they tend to be formed in childhood as promotion focus people tend to have more childhood experiences with an absence or lack of positive adult responses. Whereas prevention focus tends to have a lack of negative adult responses.

Well… personally, I like this theory but I'm a bit unsure about the defining the approaches because I believe that I am either in denial about my childhood having an absence or lack of positive adult responses, or it supports the idea that the theory is making a general claim about promotion people and I'm an outsider.

Whatever, the answer; though I still believe that I'm an outsider; it shows the importance of considering individual differences in psychological theories.

Control Theory of Self-Regulation:

This theory is interesting because this theory explains how people adhere to social norms and societal standards amongst other things.

The theory proposes that people test the self against public and private standards of behaviour. Resulting in them changing their behaviour if there's a discrepancy.

The constant testing of the self allows people to improve the self through self-regulation and self-appraisals.

In addition, people will move into a state of testing and retesting until the discrepancy is resolved.

In other words, if there is a discrepancy between your own behaviour and what the social norm is, then you will constantly change your behaviour until you meet this social norm or standard.

On the other hand, according to the debated

theory of ego depletion; this is where the ego and self-control are mental resources that can be used up; self-control cannot be maintained forever. This makes self-control more difficult.

Meaning that people might give up this process of testing and simply deviate from social norms as this is easier.

Social Comparison Theory:

As humans we are all constantly comparing each other to one another, but why do we do this?

People compare themselves to others to validate their dimensions of the self. Yet this is subjective and sometimes unrealistic.

In my life, I have compared myself against friends, family members and even other writers on occasion. Nevertheless, these social comparisons can be completely pointless as we are all different and we all have our own positives and negatives.

To objectively validate ourselves, we take part in:

- Upwards comparison- where people compare themselves to someone who is potentially better at a particular dimension.

Personally, I have compared myself to friends that have had more friendships than me in the past.

- Downward comparison- where people compare themselves to a person who is potential worse at a given dimension.

I have often compared myself to the other people in my psychology class.

- Temporal comparison- we compare ourselves to a version of ourselves in the past.

I always compare myself to what I was like before something bad happened to me and before I started to take my writing seriously because I'm proud of myself for how far I've come.

<u>Self-Maintenance Model:</u>

This model was created by Tesser (1988) and it focuses on how people maintain self-esteem when faced with upward comparison. Due to upwards comparison can make people feel sad about themselves.

Therefore, when people are faced with these difficulties, people tend to:

- Avoid the comparison person- you avoid the person, so you aren't reminded that they're better than you at something.
- Devalue dimension- you decide that it's not as important as you thought it was.

- Engage in downward comparison- this reminded you that you are better than others at something.
- Exaggeration person's ability- we exaggerate their ability, so we feel that their level is impossible to get to. In turn, this makes us feel better.

CHAPTER 7: SELF-ESTEEM

Self-esteem is very important to have as well as it is a person's subjective appraisals of the self, and it can change a lot. It is constantly moving between high and low self-esteem.

In addition, self-esteem is influenced by upbringing. For example, an authoritarian and permissive parenting style tends to lead to negative self-esteem. Whereas an authoritative style leads to high self-esteem.

<u>Sources of Self-Esteem:</u>

There a lot of sources of self-esteem and we'll investigate them more in a moment. Although I believe that it's important to have a wide range of sources of self-esteem because if one source starts to give us negative self-esteem than the other sources are more likely to cover the negativity. Maintaining positive self-esteem overall.

Sources of Self-Esteem Include:

- Internal- self-esteem depends on self-schemas, emotion and flexibility of evaluations.

In other words, self-esteem can come from what we think of ourselves and we need to be flexible in our evaluation to maintain this self-esteem.

- External sources- this is were sources like social acceptance and other factors are important.
- Sociometer theory- people are motivated to maintain high self-esteem and they do this to ensure they are socially accepted.

Contingent Self-Esteem:

This type of self-esteem is where people base their self-esteem on different factors, because as previously mentioned if self-esteem is based on a wide number of sources then this can lead to high self-esteem. Whereas if self-esteem is based on a narrow number of sources or factors then this tends to decrease self-esteem.

For example, before I was forced to leave scouting, my self-esteem was based on cooking, scouting, writing, Warhammer 40,000, reading, family and friends. Meaning that my self-esteem was based on at least seven factors.

Resulting in when I was forced out and I lost scouting and my friends. I still managed to maintain high self-esteem because I managed to draw my self-esteem from the five remaining factors.

Consequences of Self-Esteem:

Self-esteem has two major impacts on our behaviour because self-esteem can help with our mood regulation as well as it can provide us with Protection From Terror of Death.

This protection is another term for terror management theory and mortality salience. In other words, how terrified we are to know that we WILL die one day.

Additionally, research has found that people with high self-esteem deal with this fear better.

Although, if a person has low self-esteem then they are more likely to be aggressive.

This is because people with lower self-esteem are more terrified knowing that they're going to die. Leading to more aggression.

Finally, narcissistic people have very high self esteem, but this high esteem comes from an insecure place. Hence, these types of people defend their self-esteem whenever it is questioned.

Self-Presentation:

As humans are very judgmental, everyone is affected by the need to look good or look at least somewhat representable for wider society.

We manage our self-presentation through impression management. This is where we manage the impression you give others, as well as self-monitoring. This is where you control how you present yourself depending on the person and situation.

For example, when I'm alone or just with immediate family. I typically wear very casual clothes because I don't need to be concerned with self-presentation.

However, when I'm going out and going to my lectures at university. I always wear a pair of jeans in an effort to improve my self-presentation.

Drives for Self-Presentation:

Here are some motives that drive us to strategic self-presentation:

- We want to be liked.
- Make people think we're dangerous
- Makes us be seen as competent
- Makes as morally respectable
- Makes as helpless and in need of sympathy

Accuracy of Self-Knowledge:

As I briefly mentioned earlier, our self-knowledge is limited a lot of the time.

For example, people don't appear to notice when or why their own attitudes change nor do they know how a situation affects their behaviour.

Equally, people don't know why they like things and people believe factors influence their behaviour when they don't influence them.

Moreover, people don't know the extent to which we have free will as well as people have a vested interest in the self.

Finally, people are often affected by the affective forecasting error. This is when we overestimate the emotional impact that positive or negative life events have on us.

In other words, humans are awful at knowing themselves.

Motivated Social Cognition and Self:

Before we dive into this section I wanted to define social cognition.

Social cognition is the subfield of psychology that investigates how people store information that's related to other people and groups, as well as this area looks at the cognitive processes that occur and are involved in social processes.

For example, how a memory about a minor group influences and involved in a social group encounter.

We have several motivations for engaging with our social cognition and exploring the self. For instance:

- We need to find out about a topic.
- We need to have Self-esteem motivation. This acts as self-enhancement.
- Cognitive consistent also known as self-verification.
- Cognitive consistency
- We have a need to affirm control over a situation and this gives us an illusion of control.

Culture and Self:

Our last section will quickly look at Individualism and collectivism cultures. These cultures have a difference in the perception of the importance of distinctiveness, uniqueness and interdependence.

For instance, individualistic cultures would prefer high distinctiveness and interdependence. Whereas a collectivistic culture wouldn't value these characteristics as highly.

Lastly, Bi-cultural people have to deal with different cultures, and they integrate both cultures into the self. This can be challenging but very rewarding as well.

Overall, I hope that you've found it interesting and an enlightening first few chapters.

CHAPTER 8: ATTITUDES AND SOCIAL COGNITION

We all have attitudes and some of them are very interesting so in this chapter, we'll be investigating the psychology behind attitudes.

What Are Attitudes?

Attitudes are preferences and they can be positive, negative or ambivalent.

Ever since Freud, psychologists have suspected the existence of the unconscious or implicit attitude.

Ways to Measure Attitudes:

In order to measure attitudes, we have to take two main approaches.

If we are measuring explicit attitudes, then we can just ask people about their attitudes.

For example, what is your opinion on African

Americans or homosexuals?

However, if we are measuring implicit attitudes; these attitudes that are unconscious, quick to activate and hard to change; so we have to use different methods. Such as we can use electromyography (EMG) to measure the electrical activity of muscles, as well as other neuroscience techniques. Such as an electroglottograph (EEG) and a functional Magnetic Resonance Imaging (fMRI).

Values:

Our values are enduring, evaluating beliefs about general aspects of our behaviour.

For example, some of the values include:

- Integrity
- Honesty
- Kindness
- And more.

Our values can be influenced by:

- Our culture
- Our personality
- Our politics
- Our attitudes

Lastly, there are ten values that appear to be universal. Some of these ten values include power, achievement, hedonism and stimulation.

A personal example of values would be:

- Kindness
- Internationalism
- Equality
- High quality and engaging content

Ideologies:

Ideologies are more general than attitudes as well as they are interrelated and widely shared beliefs that to relate to social and political contexts.

Interestingly, we can inherit political ideologies to some extent as demonstrated by Bouchard et al (2003) that showed political conservatism seems to be inheritable.

This is probably due to the inherited difference in cognitive ability and opinion.

We look more at ideologies later in the book.

The function of attitudes:

Katz (1960) defined 4 functions of attitudes.

- Knowledge function- we want to feel like we understand the world. Including schemas that help us to make sense of the information in the social world.

- Utilitarian function- attitudes help us to obtain rewards and avoid punishment.
- Value expressive function- attitudes allow people to express their deep-seated values.
- Ego defensive function- protect us from psychological threats.

For example, my opinion about internationalism functions as a way for me to express my deep-seated values.

Whereas my opinion about being an independent author and how great it is, functions as an ego defence.

Formation of Attitudes:

When it comes to forming our own attitudes humans do not typically know how their attitudes got formed but through research. Here are some of the ways that humans form attitudes:

- Mere exposure (Zajonc, 1968)- the more exposed we are to a stimulus, the more we like it.
- Classical conditioning- simple forms of learning where negative or positive reactions are reached when paired with another stimulus.
- Instrumental conditioning
- Observational learning

- Genes (twin studies)
- Formed through the process of social interaction
- Formed by our group and cultural membership.

Attitudes tend to stick around more when they're consistent as well as being in an echo chamber and the confirmation bias can occur. This is when people seek information that supports our worldviews.

This is why it's important to read, watch or mix with other people that have different views to you as you are validated and form a more informed opinion based on these different views.

Attitude-Behaviour Link:

I suppose that it is sort of common sense to say that our attitudes must affect our behaviour to some extent. For example, our attitudes influence our voting behaviour.

An example of the attitude-behaviour link is that private self-consciousness attitudes are made more salient by looking at in a mirror. (Diener and Walborn 1976)

In other words, if you look in a mirror when walking past a charity box you are more likely to donate.

Finally, overtime as we continue to repeat the same habits and attitudes. These habits are burned into our neural pathways in our brain. Making them more difficult to overcome.

Theory of Planned Behaviour:

The combination of attitudes, subjective norms and our perceived behavioural control combine to give us our behavioural intent then a behaviour.

To see this in action please check out Health Psychology.

Embodied Social Cognition:

After looking at attitudes, we're going to be investigating another interesting as well as odd part of social psychology- embodied social cognition.

Embodied social psychology can be defined as when we feel or act what we're thinking.

For example, one odd finding is that holding a warm cup of coffee makes people like strangers more. (Lizeman and Semin, 2009)

The possible reason for this finding could be that holding something warm makes us feel good internally. Leading us to embody our internal feelings of goodness. Making us likes strangers more.

Personally, I find a lot of the findings in this area

to be impressive and I believe that these findings are *true*. It shows how impressive the human mind is.

CHAPTER 9: COGNITIVE DISSONANCE

Cognitive dissonance is a very real behaviour and I'll share an example with you in a minute.

You can define cognitive dissonance as an unpleasant psychological state which occurs when people notice their attitudes and behaviours are inconsistent.

One example of cognitive dissonance in action can be seen in Festinger (1957).

In the experiment, they got participants to take part in a boring experiment and then at the end they asked them for help and if they agreed. They were asked to convince a participant; that was a confederate; that the experiment was enjoyable.

This would mean that the participant would go through cognitive dissonance because their attitudes; the experiment was boring, and their behaviour; telling someone that it was enjoyable; didn't match,

The results for the experiment showed that the control group rated it as boring, the group that was offered one dollar for their help rated it as enjoyable because they justified their lying, not because of the tiny reward but because they changed their attitudes to match their behaviour. The group that was offered a twenty-dollar reward found it boring as they justified the lie because of the reward.

Overall, showing you that cognitive dissonance can be a powerful thing as people will always try to decrease this unpleasant feeling.

In addition, Fazio (1984) argued four factors can cause cognitive dissonance:

- People must realise the inconsistency has negative consequences.
- A person must take responsibility for their actions.
- Physiological arousal (feeling anxiety)
- The person must attribute arousal to action.

<u>People Can Reduce Cognitive Dissonance By:</u>

- Changing their attitude.
- They can reduce the importance of consistency
- They can seek self-affirmation (restoring positive self-view)
- They could consume alcohol (Steele, Southwick and Critchlow, 1981)

Finally, Heine and Lehman (2007) suggested that cognitive dissonance is common across cultures.

CHAPTER 10: SOCIAL IDENTITY THEORY

Before we continue, I must note that these shorter chapters have been updated since the first edition, as well as these shorter chapters, serve as an introduction that the larger third edition topics are based upon.

People tend to categorize the world. Whether it's who's good and bad, who's popular and everything in-between. People categorise the world.

It's commonly believed we categorise the world to reduces our cognitive load, give the world meaning and order as well as to reduce uncertainty. Because let's face it nobody enjoys uncertainty.

Even the research has shown a lack of clear and certain social identities- associated with anxiety, stress, depression and disorganised behaviour. (Durke & Reitz, 1991)

This leads us into the topic of Social Identity Theory by Tajfel & Turner (1979) and Abrams & Hoggs (1990)

Personally, I find social identity theory to be a really interesting theory as it explains why people act differently around others and it helps to explain intergroup conflict.

But the journey to understand what social identity theory is, is long so let's start our journey.

Social Identity Theory is essentially a theory about intergroup conflict so why groups fight amongst themselves, and it aims to explain why conflict, as well as discrimination, happens.

Furthermore, the theory makes six main claims. These are:

- That a group doesn't need to compete for resources for a conflict to develop.

In other words, you and your friends don't need to be competing for a mate; for example; for there to be a conflict. Like an argument to happen.

- Another claim of Social Identity Theory is that if your group perceives a member of your group to belong to another group. This would result in out-group discrimination and in-group favouritism.

This links to social categorisation. This is where you categorized people in your group (in-group) and an outgroup. (a group that isn't your own)

An example of this claim in the real world would be if your friend belonged to your group but another that you disliked. Such as, a group of friends that betrayed you. You would discriminate against them for being a part of that group and you would show favouritism to the rest of your social group.

- The third claim of this theory is that social categorisation provides you with a way of developing your social identity.

In other words, by categorising people into ingroups and outgroups we allow ourselves to develop a part of the self that we create based on our group membership.

An example of this claim would be if you belonged to the popular group at school. By categorising others as less or equally popular this allows you to form a social identity that you're popular and 'cool'

- The fourth claim is that individuals want to achieve a positive social identity because it increases self-esteem.

Therefore, you would want to be seen with the 'cool' or good social groups so you would have a positive social identity. Increasing your self-esteem.

- The penultimate claim is positive social identity is based on distinctiveness and good social comparison. (the process of comparing your group to outgroups)

An example of this is that in order to have a positive identity you would want your social group to be distinctive and better than other groups that you dislike. For instance, being better at football or science than the outgroups.

- The final claim is that when your social identity isn't positive then you will want to leave or improve the group.

In the real world, this could be if your friendship group did drugs at school and became a friendship group that was known for doing drugs. Even if it was only the once. Then you might want to leave the group so your identity would improve, or you would want and try to improve the group's identity, so your group isn't known for doing drugs anymore.

Now that you know what Social Identity Theory is, we can start to explore the evidence for it.

Personally, I believe in the theory because it's largely true, but you can't prove it even with the experiments below. Mainly because you can link an experiment to Social Identity Theory, but you can't test Social Identity Theory itself as I'll explain.

Chen et al (2005)

In this experiment, 149 bi-cultural students from a Singaporean university completed an online questionnaire.

First, they were asked what culture do they consider themselves more a part of. Their choices were American or Singaporean. This was done by showing them 12 photos that represented that culture and they were asked to try and remember as many as they could.

Then they were asked if they would pay a few more dollars to get next day delivery on a book.

Lastly, they were asked to name the first 3 politicians that came to mind.

The results showed that western cultures prefered the item right away as well as the politicians were relevant to their primed culture so priming happened throughout.

In conclusion, culture identities play a role in online shopping.

Critically Thinking:

The study was effective because it made sure that cultural priming was maintained throughout. This ensured that the culture continued to play a role in the experiment.

Nevertheless, this study was done online, and people don't tend to focus on online questionnaires so this could have been rushed. Thus, the results of this experiment may not actually represent the culture they claim to, or there may not be as clear of a difference as the results suggested.

I know from personal experiences that when I'm completing an online study at my university. It's very difficult to concentrate and after a while, the studies get very boring. Leading to people rushing them.

Tajfel (1970)

In this study, a sample of 48 boys from 12-14 years old was asked to rate 12 paintings that were done by expressionist painters Klee or Kandinsky then they were randomly allocated groups and told that they preferred one of the artists.

Subsequently, each boy was told to award one boy from his own group points and another boy from the other group. There were two systems for awarding points:

- System 1- the points were linked to give a total of 15 so as the reward for one boy increased, the other decreased. For example, if I rewarded someone by my ingroup 12 points.

The boy from the other group would only get 3 points.

- System 2- the researchers manipulated the system. If a member gave a high value for the ingroup member then it would give a higher profile for the ingroup. If the member gave an ingroup member a low score it would give the other team 1 point. Then if the ingroup member got a mid-ranged score then it would award the team the same number of points.

The results showed, using system 1 everyone gave their in-group members more points. Showing ingroup favouritism.

Using system 2- the boys were willing to give their own team fewer points to get a bigger gap between the two teams.

In conclusion, all that is needed to create discrimination is a minimal group and it shows that intergroup conflict isn't needed for discrimination to occur.

Critically Thinking:

The strength of the study is that the procedure was well controlled because of the high level of control over the confounding variable. (an outside influence that could affect the experiment)

However, this study was only done with boys, so we don't know if the same applies to girls.

Group Memberships:

To wrap up this chapter, I wanted to talk about group memberships because throughout the book and the studies above, we know group memberships are important. Also, I wanted to add that group memberships are personal identities that become the collective identity of the group.

To simplify, the members of a football team all have the personal identities of supporting a particular football team and they like playing football. Therefore, this becomes the collective identity of the group.

Another example is psychology students all have the personal identity of being interested in psychology in amongst the personal identities of school of thoughts and opinions about psychology. However, the collective identity of the psychology student group is they like and want to learn about psychology.

When Do We Use Which Identity?

Continuing with our example above, we know the psychology student population is very different and made up of differing opinions and backgrounds. Therefore, it raises the question of when do students use their psychology student group identity and when do they use their American or British identity, for example?

It depends on the importance (salience) of the identity.

Since identities can be chronically accessible. These are identities that are valued, important and frequently used aspects of the self-concept. Or they can be situationally accessible. These are aspects that are self-evident and perceptually obvious in the immediate situation.

In other words, if a psychology student was a proud American, British, etc then their identity would be chronically accessible and they would be using that identity constantly.

Whereas if the same student was attending a university event with several other students from different subjects. Then they may not use their psychology identity since it might not be situationally appropriate.

CHAPTER 11: INDIVIDUAL AND COLLECTIVE NARCISSISM

We've probably all heard of narcissism, the terrible personality trait, and all the consequences it can have on relationships.

However, we probably haven't heard of group narcissism before and it's very important to think about.

"Group narcissism is extremely important as an element giving satisfaction to the members of the group and particularly to those who have few other reasons to feel proud and worthwhile" (From, 1973, p. 275)

This is measured using the Collective Narcissism Scale by Golec de Zavala, Cichocka, Eidelson & Jayawickreme (2009)

Before we dive into group narcissism, I want to explain Individual narcissism as the distinction is critical.

Firstly, Individual narcissism is a defensive type of self-esteem that is characterized by a discrepancy between explicit and implicit self-esteem (Bosson et al., 2003; Jordan et al., 2003) as well as it's linked to extreme anger and emotional linked to extreme emotional instability (Emmons, 1987) as well as aggressiveness. (Baumeister, Bushman & Campbell, 2000)

Whereas group narcissism is an emotional investment in unrealistic beliefs about the in-group's greatness and this is often subject to chance on the external validation of others.

This occurs because certain groups feel politically powerless and alienated by other groups. (Cichocka et al., 2015)

Therefore, they form this group narcissism. For a range of reasons. Like:

- To increase how threatening others perceive them. (Cichocka & Golec de Zavala, 2011; Golec de Zavala, Cichocka et al., 2009; Golec de Zavala, Cichocka, & Iskra-Golec, 2013)
- To become more hostile in response to criticism, threat and lack of recognition (Cichocka & Golec de Zavala, 2011; Golec de Zavala, Cichocka et al., 2009; Golec de Zavala, Cichocka, & Iskra-Golec, 2013)

- To combat Prejudice (Cai & Gries, 2013; Golec de Zavala & Cichocka, 2012; Golec de Zavala, Cichocka, & Bilewicz, 2013; Lyons et al., 2010, 2013

CHAPTER 12: SOCIAL COGNITIVE THEORY

There are many reasons why I love this unit or have a great interest in this unit and one of the reasons is this amazing theory as it explains how we learn, and I just found it interesting to put a name to this obviously true theory.

Social Cognitive Theory (SCT) or Social Cognitive Learning Theory as it was once called. It's exactly that. It's the theory that we learn by observing other people and their consequences.

It's as simple as that. Well, we could go into more depth about the theory but when its essences are in the paragraph above. What's the point?

Especially, as this chapter is an introduction.

So, how can this theory be put into the real world?

The question is more how can't we apply it to the real world.

As a result, Social Cognitive Theory can be applied to many different situations. For example, speech as we observe others as babies speaking and then we try to recreate that behaviour as we have seen people perform it so we can learn from them how to speak.

Another situation is bullying we watch others bully us or other people, so we learn from them how to do it.

The final example is violence as we watch others perform violence on TV, in films or we see people in fights. From this watching, we see how to perform violence.

Bandura, Ross and Ross (1961)

The study was made up of 3-5-year-old children and their level of aggression was evaluated first, so a matched-pair design could be used to group children with similar levels of aggression together. Then the children would watch a male or female model act aggressively or passively towards the Bobo doll or as a control group they would simply be put with the bobo alone. To see what they would do to the doll.

Each child would go into a room and after seeing all the toys they would be told that they weren't allowed to play with them. Making them frustrated.

Results showed that the groups with the aggressive model shown the most aggression, then the control group and then the passive model group were the least violent. Plus, the male groups were the most violent.

Critically Thinking:

The study was well controlled as children with similar levels of aggressive behaviour were put together.

However, this experiment has ethical concerns because by introducing and teaching the children violence. How negatively are we affecting their future?

Joy, Kimball and Zabrack (1986)

They studied three towns in Canada. A town called Notel in 1973 which didn't have TV and again in 1975 when they had one TV channel.

Two other towns were observed as well but they already had a TV.

120 elementary school children were observed to do with their level of verbal and physical aggression on the playground. Peers' and teacher's ratings of the aggressions were taken as well.

Results showed that aggression dramatically increased in Notel from 1973 to 1975 whereas the other two towns didn't increase significantly over the two years. The peer and teacher ratings supported this.

The researchers found that males were more aggressive than females.

They concluded that the most likely explanation was that the children got heighten arousal from the new television and this heighten arousal led to an increase in aggression.

<u>Critically Thinking:</u>

This study's findings can be applied to general society as the findings were shown in three different locations, so we know that this is a general behavioural trend.

Saying that, as this wasn't an international study these findings can't be applied to other countries as we don't know the extent to which their culture would affect the results.

PART TWO: THE SOCIAL GROUP

CHAPTER 13: THE SOCIAL GROUP

Groups are central to human existence; without them, we can't survive and our ancestors showed us the power of these social groups. As a result, we were able to build vast cities and empires because we formed groups.

For example, the Romans joined together and started the roman empire as well as the British united to start the British Empire and we managed to conquer a third of the world, but that was a very long time ago.

In addition, groups influence who we are and how we live.

What Is a Group?

This is not a simple question because a group can be large or small, structured or unstructured, specific or general, physically close or scattered (Deaux et al, 2005) as well as groups can perhaps have a feeling of common fate (Lewis, 1948)

For example, I can feel that I am a part of the psychology student group but this group in itself is massive as it's spread national and international borders.

Another example is that I am a student and a part of the student group. This group is close to me at the university yet this group has many subgroups as well. For example, the successful and unsuccessful students, the students doing different degrees as well as the party-loving students and the non-partying students.

According to Johnson and Johnson (1987), these are the essential features of a group: interaction, people need to perceive the self as part of the group, groups need to be interdependent, they need to have a common goal, structure of norms or rules as well as the members need to influence each other, and the group need to have a joint association to satisfy a need.

Referring to my personal examples, back in secondary school or middle school. I was a part of the Warhammer 40,000 wargaming club. As a group we had a common goal; this was to play Warhammer 40,000, and we had interaction.

However, we weren't interdependent yet we were

still a group so these essential features aren't universal or cannot apply to all groups.

Two more ideas of a group definition are from Tajfel (1981) were he said: 'two or more individuals… perceive themselves to be members of the social category' and 'Us versus them' from Turner (1982)

<u>Social Identity Theorists:</u>

According to Social Identity Theorists, as discussed in a previous chapter, they define a group as two more people who themselves and are recognised by others as groups and have a sense of 'us' which can be compared to 'them' formations of groups.

This definition works as a general definition as well.

In other words, social identity theorists believe that a group is made up of two or more people and the important part of the group is that the members of this group and non-member must see this group as a group. Furthermore, the theorists state that the group has a concept of ingroup and outgroup, as discussed in the Social Identity chapter.

CHAPTER 13: FORMATION OF THE GROUP AND NORMS

According to Tuckerman (1965), there are 5 stages of group formation.

Forming is the first stage and it involves coming together, accepting each other, avoiding conflict and working out the purpose and roles of the group.

Secondly, you have the storming phase. This is where you address issues within the group. There's usually some intergroup conflict but this conflict can be supported in harmony.

After the storming stage, you have the norming stage. In this stage, the group focuses on listening, supporting and being flexible to other group members. In addition, the group usually has a common identity and a purpose by this stage.

The last two stages are the performing stage. This is where the group is very task orientated as well as adjoining is the last stage. This is when the task is completed, and the group disengages.

Group Socialisation:

Group socialisation is the process of the group and its members coming together and meeting each other's needs over time.

Moreover, the group and each individual member of the group are constantly evaluating each other to see if the group is right for them.

When it comes to group socialization, Moreland and Levine (1982) have proposed these five stages:

Firstly, a person is a prospective member of a group and they are investigating whether the group is right for them.

Afterwards, the member joins the group and starts to socialise with the group. This is when they become part of the group. The stage is being a marginal member.

Next, the member goes through the maintenance stage. This is where they are a full member and only need to maintain their standing or position in the group.

However, if a group member doesn't maintain their group membership then they may need to go through reconciliation. Where they are earning the trust of the group back and learning how to be a full member again.

On the other hand, if they fail in resocialization then they can quit the group entirely. This stage is called remembrance.

Interestingly, people being a part of a group can still be important years after they left the group. We will come back to this later in the book.

In addition, group socialisation often involves initiation rites and 'people accept negative outcomes due to cognitive dissonance' (Festinger, 1967) and as a result, they put the group in higher esteem to combat dissonance.

Interestingly, even if a person is subjected to an extremely humiliating initiation rite. It can make that person want to be a part of that group even more.

One reason for this behaviour would be that the individual wants to make sure that the act of humiliation wasn't done in vain.

Overall, groups benefit from socialisation and there's a range of socialisation outcomes that describe how the group member feel about how they function. Most commonly it is group coherence.

Forces within a group:

There are a lot of forces within a group and all

these different forces influence the group and shape the group into what the world sees.

According to Festinger et al (1950), the forces within a group are:

- The attractiveness of group members and the group. This describes the forces that make you like the group.
- Social interaction goals- does the amount of social interaction in the group meet what you're looking for.
- Individual goals- does the group help you to meet your goals.
- Individual goals interdependent with group
- Coherence- is the group united.
- Behaviour- does your behaviour adhere to the standards of the group.

Norms:

In my opinion, group norms are very interesting because all groups have them as well as each group has its own unique set of norms.

For example, in the author community, the norms are: produce high-quality work, engage with readers and be human.

Norms can be defined as the individual set of behaviour and attitudes that determine, organise and defines groups from another group.

These norms can be formal or informal but all norms regardless of the group help to regulate and guide the group's behaviour.

Furthermore, norms provide us with a frame of reference so we know how to behave in a certain group and some norms are universal, as well as some vary across cultures

Ultimately, norms can guide our behaviour in a group, but they can change attitudes and behaviour as well. Typically, this happens when we desire to be part of a certain group.

Why Do Norms Work?

Norms work for several reasons. For example, groups often encourage them, so we quickly learn the group's norms during socialisation as well as we often internalise them.

As a result, whenever we are with the group, we remember the norms and the norms become activated.

Overall, social norms act as action heuristics to make life easier.

Are Norms Good At The Group Level?

In my opinion and the research has shown that the answer is yes because Coch and French (1948) found that by permitting groups to form their own norms. They increased in the group's effectiveness because the group decided how they wanted to work.

CHAPTER 15: ROLES, GENDER AND MORE

Roles:

In this section, we're going to get into the tricky subject of social roles.

On a personal note, I don't believe in social roles. For example, I don't believe in women should be housewives and men have to be the breadwinner of the family.

Social roles are shared expectations of how people in groups are supposed to behave. For example, in my Warhammer 40,000 club, I oversaw the group, so my social role was that of the leader.

A positive about social roles is that groups with set roles tend to be more satisfied and performed better (Barley and Beckly, 2004)

Roles can sometimes make the group lose sight

of right and wrong. Especially, when these social roles seem illegitimate or arbitrary. Like: gender.

Gender Roles:

Gender roles can cause conflict as well as they can change who we are. As supported by Twenge (2001) who tracked women's social status between 1931-1993 and compared the findings with women's ratings of their own assertiveness.

The results showed that the pattern followed trends in women's social status. Meaning that social roles are linked to status.

Status:

In society and within any group different social role has different statuses as some roles are valued more than others. For example, the Head of State compared to a blue-collar worker.

These differences in status reflect social comparison within groups. (Festinger, 1954) and people often legitimise status differences. For example, men legitimising the historical and still present gender inequality.

Yet interestingly people can support systems that are unfair to them personally. (Jost and Banaji, 2004) for instance, my lecturer used the example of a poor woman with three children living in social housing.

You would probably find that that woman supports the government and the system that isn't helping her get out of poverty.

Social Creativity:

Sometimes the social groups we are a part of do negative things or they conduct themselves in a way that makes our esteem for the group decrease.

This happened to me a few years ago with scouting as some of the things that were going on in scouting made me dislike the group.

However, humans tend to prefer to maintain esteem for a group. Especially, when the group is important to us. Like how scouting was important for me.

Therefore, people engage in social creativity to help improve their esteem for a group.

Social creativity is the strategies that a person uses to improve and maintain their esteem for a group.

One strategy that people can use is focusing on another dimension. (Tajfel and Turner, 1979)

Such as We are a poor country but we are good at sports.

Group Sensitivity:

Humans can be sensitive people and the Intergroup sensitivity effect (Homer et al 2002) is when we are more likely to accept criticism if it's from the ingroup.

In my opinion, this is relatively true as I am more likely to accept criticism about a study if it's another psychology student or someone in the field of psychology compared to someone who isn't.

Optimal Distinctiveness:

It is natural for humans to want to distinguish themselves from others as well as to make themselves feel special and this is what groups can do for us. (Brewer, 1991)

For example, I want to be distinguished in the job market from the rest of my group. In this case, my group is a psychology graduate. Therefore, I want to distinguish myself by writing books and being an author.

CHAPTER 16: NEGATIVES OF SOCIAL GROUPS AND WHY GROUPS CANBE BAD FOR US?

Ostracism and Social Exclusion:

When people are excluded from things people tend to feel sad, angry and psychologically distressed. I know this from experience.

Interestingly, it hurts us even when we don't belong to the group that excludes us. (Gonsaikrale and Williams, 2007) as well as this mental pain has demonstrated in neuroscience studies to reassemble real physical pain.

Also, Ostracism has other benefits to social groups as well. Since it motivates group members to follow group norms. (Ouwerkerk et al, 2005) and it deters other groups members from following the example of the defected people. (Kerr et al, 2009)

In other words, ostracism can be about

controlling the group.

Deviants:

These types of people are marginal group members and they are generally disliked because they make it more difficult to hold the group in high esteem. Additionally, they threaten the positive image of the ingroup. (Marques et al, 2001)

For example, if a few members of the church decide to start attacking non-Christians then these deviants most certainly threaten the positive image of Christianity.

On the other hand, deviants can be good for the group because they can point out things that are wrong with the group so they can be improved. (Parker, 2008, 2010)

Imposters:

This is a new but interesting area of research that examines how imposters affect the social group and Jetten et al (2005) presented vegetarians with meat eaters and when one of the vegetarian group members was caught eating meat. The group dealt with them harsher than the outgroup members.

Schism:

This is when the group breaks off and these smaller groups form their own subgroups.

In addition, subgroups can engage in cross-cutting. In essence, this is when these subgroups include and mix with other people that aren't apart of the larger group.

The easiest example of crosscutting would be if a subgroup of the UK Conservative Political Party decided to include members of a subgroup of the Labour Party into their numbers.

When Might Groups Be Bad for You:

Another common theme of the book is social groups aren't always good for you because if you're apart of a stigmatised group. Then this can have several side effects. Like: prejudice.

Also, belonging to a stigmatised group can negatively affect well-being (Markowitz, 1998: Link & Phelan, 2006)

Subsequently, social groups can be bad for people if the group has unhealthy group norms. Like: criminal activity is normal and encouraged.

Nevertheless, social groups aren't cut and dry good or bad because people can still want to be a part of groups that are considered bad for them.

For instance, if you're being bullied or ostracised from a group then you might still want to be a part of a group. Due to the group still having important qualities and friendships for you.

And this is before we consider the palliative effects for people being a part of a social group. Let alone a stigmatised group.

In short, sometimes people prefer to be in a social group that isn't ideal. Rather than being without a social group at all.

This links back into the terror management and other social group benefits discussed early in the book.

I know it's complicated, but this is why social psychology is a great subfield of psychology that I love.

CHAPTER 17: GROUP DECISION MAKING AND THE HIDDEN PRODILE

Our next topic about social groups has to involve decision because a lot of our lives depend on the decisions of groups. Whether it be laws or job acceptance, we rely on group decisions.

Also, we make a lot of decisions in groups. For example, what to eat or where to go on holiday.

Does Unique Knowledge Contribute to Group Decisions?

The answer to this question is mainly about the phenomenon known as the Hidden Profile Problem.

This was actually my first statistic project at university.

So, the Hidden Profile Problem can be simply defined as the problem that occurs when some information is shared in the group and other information is not.

Whilst, the above is a simplification of the problem, you'll learn it's complexities throughout the section.

We all have collective knowledge that everyone knows. Then we all have private, unique pieces of information.

And this is the essence of the Hidden profile Problem.

Does Unique Information Get Considered When Groups Make Decisions?

According to Stasser & Titus (1985, 1987), it does because new unique arguments can be the most persuasive in decision making.

On the other hand, it doesn't get considered because groups tend to focus on information that everyone has compared to information that is uniquely known to certain people. (Stasser & Titus, 1985, 1987, 2003)

Furthermore, groups focus too much on common information and insights and don't discuss information that is unique to one person or the minority. (Stasser, 1992, Stasser & Stewart, 1992)

Even when bits of unique information are voiced, they tend to be ignored, not understood or integrated into the decision. (Dennis, 1996; Kerr &

Tindal, 2004; Larson et al, 1994)

This is a problem because failure to disclose and attend to hidden profile information tends to result in a poorer quality decision. (Dennise, 1996; Stasser & Titus 1985)

CHAPTER 18: WHY THE HIDDEN PROFILE OCCURS AND HOW TO OVERCOME IT?

The problem occurs for many reasons.

For example, time is one factor because time pressure puts more urgency on closure. This makes the participants less receptive to a diverging discomforting perspective. (Kerr & Tindalle, 2004)

Yet they are more focused on the task because of the time pressure. (Karan & Kelley, 1992)

You could say it's weighting up do you want your team to make the correct decision or do you want them focused?

Another factor is group size because the larger the group, the higher the chance that individual ideas and insights will be overlooked. (Steiner, 1972)

Large group diversity is another factor because

the greater group diversity, the more likely there will be intergroup conflicts and stereotypes will compromise the full utilisation of vendor resources. (Cariso & Wolley, 2008)

Additionally, shifts in group composition can cause the Hidden Profile Problem because the more frequently the group composition changes the harder it is for its members to keep track of which members have unique or relevant information or expertise. (Lewis et al 2007)

Penultimately, groups that are geographically dispersed and rely on electronic technology can cause the hidden Profile as more dispersed groups rely more on electronic technology for communication. This makes it more challenging for members to get a guarded take on who knows what. (Nemiro et al, 2018)

I think we know this is true because when I'm talking to my friends about a university project. There have definitely been times when I would have rather called them. Since telling them what they need to know is difficult in a text message.

On the other hand, for University group projects when we're talking on WhatsApp, it's difficult to know who knows what. So, I tend to explain it like they know nothing.

Thankfully, it helps people and they aren't offended.

Finally, social costs and status can cause the Hidden Profile to occur due to some studies has found higher status members of the medical team, for example, are more likely to discuss unique information compared to lower status members.

It's riskier for lower status members to share unique information over credibility concerns. (Stewart & Stasser, 1995

How Can Groups Overcome the Hidden Profile Problem?

According to Bauran & Bonner (2004) and Stewart & Stasser (1995) people must recognise other members have special information or expertise relevant to the group's tasks.

Then the group needs to value these members who contribute. (Caruso & Wolley, 2008)

Finally, the group must be motivated and coordinated to actually use member resources. (Quigley et al, 2007)

Of course, this is a lot harder than it sounds because the group would have to overcome a number of factors. Like: differences in the status of members, intergroup bias, stereotypes and more.

Therefore, one way to overcome these difficulties to make all members of the group have equal status. (Hollingshead, 1996)

I'll leave you to consider the practicalities of this idea.

Do Groups Make Better Decisions Than Individuals?

Theoretically speaking, you would assume groups make better decisions because there are more people with different backgrounds and ideas.

The reality is very different and a popular way of researching this area is by brainstorming.

This is the generation of novel ideas groups member generate as many as quickly as possible. (Osborn, 1957)

Yet Diehl and Stroebre (1987) suggest there is little evidence that individual brainstorming in groups are more creative than alone.

However, eyewitness testimony is more accurate when a group account is given compared to individual reports. (Warnick & Saunders, 1980)

Finally, when groups work together and critique each other's work. It produces better work. (McGlynn et al, 2004)

Personally, this is an interesting mixture of

results and even the McGlynn isn't true all of the time. Since the exact opposite is true when it comes to writing.

This Could Be Down to Four Reasons:

- Evaluation apprehension- results in people withholding ideas from the group.

I've certainly done this a number of times when I've been in groups.

- Social loafing and free riding- allowing certain people to create the bulk of the ideas.

This always happens to me when I'm in a group.

- Production matching- when people brainstorm alone their production rate depends on individual differences. But in groups, it depends on comparison with other members. Therefore, this leads to matching our performance based on the output of other members.
- Blocking- not being able to speak when others are talking. Leading to people forgetting ideas and it reduces productivity.

How to Overcome Drawbacks to Brainstorming?

After seeing the negatives of group brainstorming, we need to see how groups can overcome these problems.

Firstly, groups can combine individual and group brainstorming. (Brown & Paulis, 2002) to generate the most ideas, as well as you get the best of both worlds.

Another idea is to have the group members communicate in writing. (Mullen, Johnson & Jalas, 1991) this prevents people from forgetting ideas and prevents the blocking problem.

The same logic works on electronic brainstorming where groups use computers to produce more ideas. (Gallupe et al, 1994)

Moreover, making a helegenous groups; where members have diverse knowledge types and backgrounds, may lead to a stimulating environment to produce more ideas. (Stroebe and Diehl, 1994)

Finally, people believe group brainstorming works because of the Illusion of group effect. (Stroebe and Diehl, 1994) And as we know from earlier people make more ideas alone.)

CHAPTER 19: GROUP MEMORY AND THE GROUP THINK PHENOMENON

To finish up this section on group decision making, we need to talk about the group memory and how bad it is as well as the interesting thing known as Group Think.

If you want to learn more about memory, how it works and how unreliable it can be. I recommend you check out Cognitive Psychology.

Group Memory:

When it comes to remembering information, Clark and Stephenson (1989, 1995) found groups tend to remember more information than individuals.

As well as Lorge and Solomon (1995) found groups recall more because individuals communicate unshared information and because their group recognises true information when they hear it.

However, this idea of better information recall

depends on the memory tasks because Steiner (1976) found groups remember more on simplistic artificial tasks. (like nonsense words) than complex realistic tasks.

Group Think:

Group think is a desire to reach a unanimous decision can override the motivation to reach a proper rational decision-making process. (Janus, 1972)

As well as Group Think can be used to explain the USA's failure to predict Pearl Harbour and the escalation of the Vietnam war.

A Group Can Be Especially Vulnerable to Group Think:

- When members have similar backgrounds.
- Group is insulated from outside opinions.
- No clear rules for decision making.
- Collective rationalization Members discount warnings and do not reconsider their assumptions because of their belief in inherent morality.
- Stereotyped views of out-groups.

In other words, the group believes outgroups don't know what they're talking about.

- Illusion of unanimity- The majority view and judgments are assumed to be unanimous.

Therefore, the group believes if one person thinks it then everyone must think it.

- Self-appointed 'mindguards'

I know this sounds like a strange reason for Group Think but this is when members protect the leader and the group from information that would prove problematic or contradicts the group's view, cohesiveness, and decisions.

- Illusion of invulnerability

Lastly, this can create Group Think because this creates excessive optimism in the group that encourages them to take extreme risks.

<u>Preventing Group Think:</u>

Janis (1982) proposes a few ideas about how Group Think can be prevented. These include:

- The Leader assigning someone to be devil's advocate and critically evaluate each idea.
- The groups and their leaders should avoid stating preferences and expectations at the outset.
- Everyone should be encouraged to critically think about the ideas.

- An expert should be invited to meetings regularly to challenge and critique ideas.
- Everyone in the group should discuss the ideas with a trusted friend or family member to report back to the group and their reaction.

The majority of these ideas help to combat the group being insulated from outside opinion and members having similar backgrounds.

However, much of the research on Group Think is retrospective, as well as there is an inconsistency in findings.

For example, Rovio, Eskola, Kozub et al (1996) found high group cohesion led to a pressure to conform. Resulting in Group Think and a reduction in performance.

Whereas Postmes, Spears & Cihangir (2001) found group cohesion doesn't always lead to Group Think. Since norms of critical thought can still lead to the correct decision being made.

PART THREE: INTERGROUP RELATIONSHIPS

CHAPTER 20: INTERGROUP RELATIONS AND STEREOTYPES

In this chapter, we'll be investigating how the relationships within and outside a group affect behaviour.

Here are some key terms that are needed for this topic:

- Stereotype- these are simplified but widely shared beliefs about the characteristics of a group and its members.
- Prejudice- negative affective reactions to a group.
- Discrimination- others treat a person worse because of their group membership.

<u>Cognitive Misers:</u>

People are seen as cognitive misers because people believe that there is not enough space in the working memory to process everyone as an individual.

Therefore, people rely on shortcuts or heuristics. (Fische and Taylor, 1991) These shortcuts include stereotyping others.

The human miser approach argues that people use stereotypes as mental shortcuts because they don't have enough mental resources to treat everyone as an individual.

As a result, people typically have less contact with minority or other groups other than their own. This can lead to the overestimation of the negative characteristics of the group.

Although, stereotyping and prejudice are affected by how people want to think as well because dogmatic individuals, individuals who need structure and people who need cognitive closure, all tend to stereotype and be prejudice more.

Cognitive limitations:

Throughout the series, I have shown you that humans have a number of cognitive limitations as people draw on stereotypes to gain knowledge about people they barely know. (Ditser and Koorman, 1996)

Category Accentuation:

It turns out that the mere act of categorisation can distort the perception of groups. For example, if I place the group of foster children into a positive category then my perception is always likely to be positively biased towards them, and in reality, it is positively biased toward them due to a friendship I had.

In addition, Tajfel and Wikes (1963) found differences between categories as differences between the ingroup and outgroup are maximised and differences within the ingroup are minimized.

In other words, when I group children together like foster children, clinically normal and autistic children. I am more likely to group the characteristics of these groups as similar as possible and maximizing the differences between my children and adult groups.

Stereotypes

We are all guilty of having stereotypes about people. Whether it's blonds are stupid, the French are rude or foster children are always bad. We all have stereotypes about a group of people to a lesser or greater extent than others.

A stereotype is a preconceived notion or idea about a group of people. Like in the examples above

Although, unlike prejudice; which are attitudes; and discrimination; which is a behaviour; stereotypes are meant to generalize about a group.

One of the theories about the formation of stereotypes in its simplest terms; as it's a bit long and complex; is the Illusory Correlation formed by Hamilton and Gifford (1976)

Illusory Correlation Bias:

The illusory correlation bias is a 'trick of the mind' that leads people to believe that the behaviour is more common among a minority. (Fielder, 2004) as well as it can explain why some behaviours are unfairly perceived as more characteristics of a minority even if there's a kernel of truth. (McGarly et al, 1990)

For example, the disgraceful stereotype of all Muslims are terrorists technically has a kennel of truth within it as the 9/11 attackers were Muslims. Yet this shouldn't justify this over-generalisation.

Dependency and Stereotypes:

Interestingly, when you depend on another person we tend to use stereotypes less and cognition more. Meaning that the accuracy of your opinions are more important, as well as outcome dependent people ascribed less stereotypical traits.

This is probably because stereotypes can offend others so to avoid the person we depend upon turning against us. We take the extra time to use our condition instead of these metal shortcuts.

However, this is only when we are not cognitively busy. (Pendy and MacRae, 1994)

Some further evidence of stereotypes involves stereotype threat. This is when a situation can potentially confirm a stereotype. The study we'll look at involves the stereotype that black people aren't as intelligent as white people.

We'll look at the self-fulfilling prophecy as well. This is when a change in someone's expectations of someone causes a change in the behaviour of the individual.

Steele and Aronson (1995):

Black and white university students were given a 30-minute verbal test that most of the participants found challenging enough.

In the experimental group, they were told that the test was to test their verbal abilities and limitations.

In the control group, they were told that the test had nothing to do with intelligential abilities.

By linking the test to abilities, they were hoping to activate racial stereotypes so black people would feel the threat of fulfilling the stereotype.

Results showed that white and black subjects did as well as each other in the control group but the black subjects did worse than white people in the experimental group.

In conclusion, by linking the test to performance it depresses black subjects through stereotype threat but when it's not linked to ability the black subjects' performance improve and matches those of white people. This could be because of black students' apprehension to the possible conform to the stereotype.

Critically Thinking:

The study has high ecological validity; it can be applied to the real world; as it used an everyday and probable situation that students would encounter in the real world, at least when at university.

Yet the study has possible ethical concerns as it's possible that the black students were in distress because of the stereotype threat.

Rosenthal and Jacobson (1968)

Teachers were told that certain students were going to be growth-sputters because of their result in a fictional IQ test. The growth-sputters were chosen at random.

The results showed that in the year of the experiment, students that were in the control group; the non-growth sputters; increased in IQ by 8.4

points on average but the growth sputters increased by 12.2 IQ points.

In conclusion, changes in the teacher's expectation produced changes in the students' achievement, stereotypes we have about people may affect other's behaviour because of a self-fulfilling prophecy.

Critically Thinking:

The study has strong internal validity as they managed to successfully measure the effects of the self-fulfilling prophecy.

However, the study was only done in one location so it's unknown if the results could be applied to the rest of the country, let alone other cultures.

CHAPTER 21: THE OUTGROUP

I know the Outgroup is mentioned a lot in the book and it is a vital topic in social psychology. Hence, I gave it its own chapter.

Outgroup Homogeneity Effect:

In groups, people tend to see members within the same or another group as being more similar to themselves.

For instance, I see members of the university student group as more like me than a group of 60-year-old bikers.

During this homogeneity process, people tend to exaggerate the ingroup differences to the outgroup

Contrast to this effect people are more familiar with the ingroup, so we are more able to think of examples to perceive the group as diverse. (Linvile, Salovey and Fischer, 1986)

One example of this effect would be that an outsider might say that the student group is very similar or the same. However, as a member of this group, I know that the student group is very diverse. As students come from very different socioeconomic backgrounds, countries, ethnicities, regions of the country, sexual orientations and many more…

Outgroup Favouritism:

Interestingly enough, outgroup favouritism is a common factor in intergroup relations and I know from personal experience that it's real.

Since I'm not European, I'm British by birth, but in my heart, I class myself as European.

You can define outgroup favouritism as an "evaluative preference for groups to which one does not belong," (Jost et al, 2004; p, 891)

Although, explicit outgroup favouritism is relatively rare, and as a result of this, we need to test implicit attitudes. Since they play a role since we can't trust everything people say.

Meaning we need to use the Implicit Attitudes Test (IAT) invented by Greenwalfd and Danaji (1995) and it measures the subconscious and reaction time tasks.

For instance, if you show white Americans a pair

of pictures of the target group (white Americans vs African Americans) will either good or bad words.

The test measures how quickly people respond to the ingroup stimuli which is associated with good and the outgroup which is associated with bad. Compared to vice versa.

Why Is Outgroup Favouritism Important?

Overall, outgroup favouritism is important because it goes against theories that say people are motivated solely by their own interests or the interests of the group.

Especially, low-status groups that show implicit outgroup favouritism towards high-status groups.

Personally, I think this is an interesting point because theoretically speaking we would only show preference for our ingroup and we should hate the outgroups.

Yet for some reason we like outgroups in certain contexts.

For example, towards the end of December 2020 with the whole Brexit situation, I was showing a strong preference for the European outgroups. Because I preferred how Europe was acting in the fight against COVID-19 amongst other things.

Yet according to the majority of social

psychology theories, I should not have had a preference for Europe since that's the outgroup.

It's interesting.

Justification Theory:

Before we pivot to the ideology section of the book, we need to talk about how people justify inequalities and intergroup relations.

Due to people can justify it by their own self-interest. (ego justification) Like: "I don't want women to be good leaders because I want the job)

Or it can be justified by group interest and group justification. For instance, "Black people can't do that job because white people might be threatened,"

Finally, intergroup relations can be justified by systems and the central idea of this justification is people have a motivation to view the social and political systems under which they live as being just and fair.

Even if they're personally disadvantaged by those systems. This is because these systems provide certainty, structure and belonging.

And this all happens because of people's ideologies.

CHAPTER 22: IDEOLOGIES

Building upon a previous chapter, ideologies are a core part of being human and we all have differing ideologies. And this is the reason why we must talk about them in this next chapter of the book.

Therefore, ideologies are an interrelated set of beliefs that give people a framework for understanding their own complex social world. (Jost et al, 2009) and the entire point of ideologies are to attempt to explain why society is the way it is.

These ideologies exist in many places. For example, in the public discourse, in media, political communication propagated by leaders and titles amongst other places

In other words, ideologies are everywhere to help us understand the social world.

Yet the most important aspect of ideologies is that people take up ideologies in order to meet their own needs for certainty, this is done through the person's own knowledge of the world, security, this is done by minimising existential threats to the person and meeting the need for belongingness. This is achieved through relational means.

For instance, having a common ideology amongst your friends and family means you can have something in common to build your relationship around.

Marxist Theory:

Furthermore, the Marxist theory of ideologies proposes that different classes have different conflicting interests, as well as class conflict stems from a ruling class exposited a lower class.

Furthermore, an equal class system is presented by a false consensus of by working hard you get to where you need to be.

Ideology plays a part in stereotyping as well because people who have more of an authoritarianism personality and score higher on the right-wing political scale tend to show more prejudice.

Social Dominance Orientation

Social dominance is the preference for hierarchy and for your group to be dominant.

According to Sudanius and Patto (1999) people

with high Social Dominance Orientation favour status hierarchies and they are much more likely to endorse prejudice against those with less social dominance. Like: minority ethnicity, racism, sexism and other non-egalitarian; equality; attitudes.

Realistic Group Conflict Theory:

This theory focuses on the struggle for material welfare. For example, food, water and land and this theory is influenced by social identity as well. As a result, both theories refer to processes at the group level.

Therefore, Sherif (1961) decided to test his theory by creating the Robbers cave study.

In the experiment, he got 11-year-old boys to form an attachment to their new groups at the summer camp they were attending (phase 1) using the minimal group paradigm (Tajfel et al,1970) then there was fierce intergroup competition. This competition resulted in physical fights between the boys. (Phase 2) finally, there was group reconciliation were the boys' conflict was reduced.

Overall, the study showed that the conflict between groups is caused by the competition for scarce resources, as well as contact and superordinate goals can reduce conflict.

The introduction of superordinate goals reduced

the conflict because it used ethnocentrism. Meaning that instead of focusing on their group and themselves the boys had to focus on the other group as well.

Race and Ethnicity:

Typically speaking, the average person has less contact with a minority group than another gender group. This leads to less knowledge about the group and it leads to stereotyping, prejudice and discrimination.

Even worse, people tend to dehumanise minority group, and this tends to legitimate worse actions against them. (Hasiam, 2006)

For example, someone stabs a black man because he was less than human.

Another awful example of dehumanisation is the historical or not as historical as we would like belief that black people are genetically inferior to white people.

Overall, it is these predominant beliefs about perceived differences between groups that ultimately leads to conflict.

Moral Credentialing:

People show more prejudice after having the opportunity to demonstrate they are not prejudice.

(Monin and Miller, 2001) then they will be more prejudice later.

Modern racism:

Some people say that racism is no more.

I would like to believe this fact but it's a lie.

Whilst, old-fashioned racism MIGHT have been driven away as white people beating up black people doesn't happen as often as it used to. It has been replaced with a more subtle form of racism.

This subtle form of racism is still a problem because it may lead to aversive racism as well as avoiding ethnic minorities.

Ageism:

Another type of prejudice is ageism because older people face many forms of prejudice. (Age Concern, 2006)

Furthermore, Levy et al (2009) did an experiment to see the effects of ageism.

As a result, 25% of all people who endorsed the ageist stereotypes had a cardiovascular event within 30 years compared to only 13% of those who didn't endorse ageist remarks.

Meaning that believing in ageism is bad for you and society as well as if you believe in karma then this is a bit more proof for you. I don't believe in karma, but the study is still interesting.

Marriage Equality:

Having an attitude that makes you against gay marriage varies according to your age and political orientation.

In my opinion, I know this first-hand because as a young person I am fine with homosexuality but my parents support homosexuality less and my grandparents support it even less.

Yet as with all social wrongs, it improves over time. For example, the Civil partnership act was met by 86% public opposition in 2002 but in 2012 Marriage equality was only opposed by 24%.

Therefore, if there are any homosexuals reading this book and are struggling with non-accepting parents or community. My advice to you is to give them time and just be yourself.

CHAPTER 23: INTRODUCTION TO SEXISM

We'll go into sexism in more depth in the next chapter but it's worth introducing the topic here.

Unfortunately, in society women are generally treated wrong and they are often faced with the battle of the sexes. Although, they are often liked more and seen as nicer than men. (Fiske et al, 2002)

Moreover, prejudice and discrimination do not always go hand in hand because you can have a prejudice against women but not discriminate. This links back to the beginning of the chapter as prejudice is the affective/emotional behaviour but discrimination is the carrying out of the behaviour and treating that person worse.

Personally, I found this section interesting because there are two types of sexism.

The first type of sexism is Hostile sexism where

women pose a perceived threat to a man's position and tend to endorse hostility more.

Subsequently, the second type of sexism is called: Benevolent sexism. This is when people have the 'Women are wonderful' stereotypes as well as 'Women are wonderful because they are necessary for men's happiness' attitudes towards women. Therefore, these attitudes are ambivalent. (Glick and Fiske, 1996)

I found this interesting because I didn't perceive this as sexism because I have known people who do think like this.

However, this type of sexism is still negative because benevolent attitudes justify women's consignment to a subordinate role. Like: caring roles as they believe that women are not suited to status-driven roles.

Additional Pitfalls of Benevolent Sexism:

- Benevolent sexists are more likely to restrain pregnant women's freedom. (Sutton et al, 2011)
- Sexists benevolent are likely to blame date rape victims. (Viki and Abrams, 2002)

How is Sexism Related to Biology?

Sexism appears to be related to biological to

some extent because objectification; for example; is when women are viewed as if their bodies represented who they are is used to equate women to their bodies.

In addition, face-ism (Archer et al, 1983) is a type of objectification because a women's physically attractive face is depictured in advertisements as objects as well.

Finally, this process of objectification changes how women behave and perceive themselves. As objectification theory proposes that objectification leads to self-objectification (Cialogue, 2004) and it is linked to the severe need for thinness to the point of being extremely thin.

CHAPTER 24: SEXISM

Whilst, I consider myself as a male to be the worse person to talk about sexism. I want to say upfront sexism is disgraceful and no women should be treated differently because of their gender.

That is disgraceful and should never be tolerated.

Moving into the psychology of sexism, there are three existing social realities that are meant to justify sexism. They are:

- Male dominance-men are the best so women are beneath them.
- Biological differences- men are stronger and have superior biology.
- Heterosexual intimacy- there is no winner of the battle of sexes because women need men.

This links into this disgusting quote when Henry Kissinger pithily said: "nobody will ever win the battle of the sexes. There's too much fraternising with the enemy."

There's the social reality in a nutshell.

In addition, sexism seems to be quite different from other types of intergroup relations. Due to its prejudice and discriminatory nature.

Also, gender relations differs from other groups relations because there's a fundamental difference between men and women.

What Is Sexism?

This clichomous perception of women should result in.

- Subjectively negative attitudes towards women seen as competitive or existing with men.
- Subjectively positive attitudes toward women seen as conforming over fitting the traditional gender roles that support and don't conflict with men.

Types of Sexism:

Hostile Sexism:

Our first type of sexism is the type of sexism that comes to mind when someone thinks of sexism, hostile sexism represents an overt justification of, or attempt, to preserve male dominance.

Hostile sexism is strongly adversarial in tone and expresses hostility toward women who are seen as rebelling or failing to conform to traditional roles.

Again, this is wrong because traditional roles are... Well, traditional and traditions need to be updated, and women should get the chance to choose what they want. Therefore, they shouldn't be lessened to a simple gender role.

Some examples of this type of sexism would be:

- "Women shouldn't be leaders,"
- "Women belong in the kitchen,"
- "Women are objects,"

<u>Benevolent Sexism:</u>

Now, this is going to be the main type of sexism we focus on in the book since some people don't see this as sexism.

Therefore, benevolent sexism seems to celebrate the intimate interdependence between men and women in a subjectively positive even adorning way. As well as this reflects a paternalize attitude that position women as weaker but nicer than men.

<u>Is This Type Really Sexism?</u>

I want to be the first person to say yes it is and you'll see the damaging effects this can have in a moment.

Yet the research supports this as well since Glick & Fiske (2001) found subjectively positive attitudes about subordinate groups can have far from positive outcomes.

Due to this can benefit some women in the short term but it negatively affects all women over time.

Although, women tend to prefer to be discriminated in benevolent sexists ways far more than hostile sexist ways.

Yet women prefer non-sexist men best. (Killianski & Rudras, 1998)

That makes sense!

What is Prejudice?

We've discussed this in other chapters but let's recap. According to Allport (1954) "an unfavourable attitude towards a social group and its members,"

And a better revised definition of prejudice is:

"Prejudice (and sexism) are relevant to our understanding of discrimination and inequality because they *legitimate actual social practices and policy;* phenomena that directly affect levels of discrimination and inequality, both in terms of prescribed social roles and in terms of unequal access to resources, status, and power at the systemic level,"

As a result, according to this perspective both prejudice and sexism need to be evaluated by their effect on a group, and only if the beliefs have a negative impact can it be called prejudice.

Instead of prejudice being simply defined as subjectively negative evaluations of a particular social group.

Is 'Benevolent Sexism' Sexist?

In theory, it isn't. If we only consider prejudice to be negative attitudes because benevolent sexism as 'positive' attitudes towards women.

On the other hand, if you define prejudice more broadly to include the role of ideologies that justify and promote inequalities then yes. Benevolent sexism is definitely sexist.

Moreover, people who are high in Benevolent Sexism tend to be high in Hostile sexism. As well as there's evidence that Benevolent Sexism causes an increase in Hostile Sexism.

In addition, women tend to endorse Benevolent Sexism more in countries with high Gender Inequality and where men are high in Hostile Sexism. This suggests a sort of 'protection-racket' effect.

This effect is believed to be because this type of sexism seems to be 'nice' and unobjectionable. Also, Benevolent Sexism undermines women's resistance to inequality and partner's control in certain contexts.

Therefore, by endorsing Benevolent sexism, it seems to shape women's goals both in terms of career and partner preferences.

Yet benevolent sexism can be used to justify extremely negative behaviour. For example, rape in some circumstances

So, I think it's fair to say benevolent sexism is far from positive.

Nonetheless, we can take this further because Sibley et al (2007) found across different nations benevolent and hostile sexism tend to positively correlate. Such as: r= 0.3 in men and r= 0.4 in women.

This is further supported by Glick et al (2002) who measured men's and women's levels of benevolent sexism in 19 countries.

They found men were higher in hostile sexism but women were higher in benevolent sexism in 6 nations.

Leading us onto our next section!

The Idea of a Protection Racket:

In the last few sections, I've talked about women being sexist in themselves. This seems counterproductive at first but it is all about protection.

Consequently, women endorse benevolent sexism more in nations men endorse hostile sexism more and there was higher inequality.

Also, Glick et al (2001) argue women could endorse benevolent sexism in these nations for its protection values.

As in these nations, the options are limited for women and women might be forced to support benevolent sexism because the risk of rebelling against the system is too high.

Yet having a high-status partner can provide more protection in these nations so benevolent sexism in women can predict increased desire for high-status partner. (0.24 vs 0.07)

Whereas hostile sexism in men predicts increased desire for an attractive partner. (r= 0.20 vs 0.7 for women)

<u>Couple Justification:</u>

To wrap up this section, I want to talk about a study that shows the dark side of benevolent sexism.

Therefore, Moyna et al. (2007) got women doing psychology and their male partners and invited them into the lab. Then the women were told they fit the profile to take part in training for working with men convicted of partner abuse.

Afterwards, the male partner got taken aside and they were told about the true nature of the study.

They were asked to present their partner with one of three reasons for not wanting them to do it. The reasons were:

- No justification condition.
- Hostile justification
- Personalized protective justification

The researchers measured the woman's response to their partner. Such as: cherished, flattered or how protected they felt.

In the no-justification condition, the note stated, "I would tell her that she cannot do this. I think it is a bad idea. Even if she thought she really wanted to do it, I would get her not to. I am sure I could convince her."

In the hostile justification condition, the note read, "I would tell her that she cannot do this. I think it is a bad idea because this is not a situation in which a woman, compared to a man, could be effective. Even if she thought she really wanted to do it, I would get her not to because a woman shouldn't get in these situations when there are men that can handle it much better. I am sure I could convince her."

In the personalized protective justification condition, the note stated, "I would tell her that she cannot do this. I think it is a bad idea because it would not be safe for her and I think she would find it to be really stressful. Even if she thought she really wanted to do it, I would get her not to because I would be very worried about her safety and well-being in this situation. I am sure I could convince her."

The results showed an ambiguous response seems to be interpreted differently by women depending on their level of Benevolent Sexism.

Meaning in the No-Justification condition, women seemed willing to trade some degree of independence based on their level of Benevolent Sexism.

Now, I want to add in about the dark side of Benevolent sexism because levels of benevolent sexism can extremely negative attitudes toward women who are seen as not fitting a 'cherished subtype'

Since men high in Benevolent sexism tend to believe that women should be cherished and protected by men. Yet this only refers to women who fit that schema (mental image) of being 'good and pure'.

If women don't fit that mental image then as I mentioned earlier hostile sexism will increase towards that 'bad and unpure' woman.

Conclusion:

This isn't going to be a psychology-based conclusion because I like to think people buy my books for my opinions and experience, as well as the information.

However, I have to say that I feel sorry for women who are exposed to sexism because it is wrong, and no woman should experience it.

So, I want to people to know that things will hopefully continue to improve over time and let's keep challenging sexism when we encounter it.

That is the only way how things will change for the better.

CHAPTER 25: IDEOLOGY OF MERITOCRACY AND WHY IDEOLOGIES ARE IMPORTANT?

One example of ideology is the idea of meritocracy. This is the idea that success should be based on merit, and I think in a 'fair' world this would be true.

Because only by working hard and smart should people be able to succeed.

However, in the real world, this is not the case because people can work extremely hard and not be successful.

Thus, this ideology believes society is currently set up so success is entirely dependent on merit, and by extension, this ideology believes:

- Those who are at the top deserve to be there.

- Those at the bottom are there because they aren't good enough.
- Disadvantaged groups aren't disadvantaged and these disadvantages are only excuses for not being good enough.
- Individual worth is the only thing that matters.

So, as you can see this is far from perfect and it isn't true because I have heard plenty of stories in the author community and the wider world where people have worked really hard and got nowhere.

Meritocracy: Palliate Effects

If this ideology helps people to justify the systems in their social world then the following should help fulfil psychological needs:

- Subscribing to these ideologies should increase well-being
- More so for people living in condition of high inequality
- Among both high and low-status groups.

Ideology Matters:

Ideologies are important for several reasons because we need to understand the role of ideologies in social processes. As prejudice cannot be understood merely as loving the ingroup and hating outgroups.

Consequently, prejudice should be thought of in terms of the beliefs systems of ideologies that allow people to justify inequality in society and we need to think about how to combat these ideologies to promote equality.

These beliefs include the ideologies of who benefit from existing inequalities and by those who are disadvantaged by them.

Moreover, they allow dominant groups to maintain control without as much resistance from subordinate groups as one might expect

However, ideologies are important because they help to fulfil people's psychological needs.

Two Quotes of Interest:

To wrap up this section on ideologies, I want to leave you with two quotes, and I would like you to think about them.

I thought they were interesting and possibly scary to say the least.

"Society's tendency is to maintain what has been. Rebellion is only an occasional reaction to suffering in human history; we have infinitely more instances of forbearance to exploitation, and submission to authority, than we have examples of revolt. Measure the number of peasant insurrections against the centuries of serfdom in Europe—the millennia of

landlordism in the East; match the number of slave revolts in America with the record of those millions who went through their lifetimes of toil without outward protest. What we should be most concerned about is not some natural tendency towards violent uprising, but rather the inclination of people, faced with an overwhelming environment, to submit to it." (Zinn, 1968; p. 16–17)

"All experience hath shewn that [hu]mankind are more disposed to suffer, while evils are sufferable, than to right themselves by abolishing the forms to which they are accustomed."

-United States Declaration of Independence, 1778

CHAPTER 26: IMPROVING INTERGROUP RELATIONS

Over the course of this section, we've investigated intergroup relations including the negatives. Like: sexism and racism.

So, I want to end this section on a more positive note and explain how social psychology can be used to improve intergroup relations.

In other words, how to combat sexism, racism and all the other negative intergroup relations.

<u>Tokenism and Affirmative Action:</u>

Personally, I think this is an interesting idea because at first, this sounds like a good idea but after reading you'll probably agree that it's a bad idea.

So, tokenism can be defined as favouring members of a minority group over majority groups in isolated episodes.

Then affirmative action can be defined as small gestures to help a particular member or members of a disadvantaged group.

In other words, this is when you hire someone not because you want them or they're good at their job. But because you don't want to be seen as sexist, racist, etc.

Yet this can purposefully or accidentally be used to hide prejudice.

Like: "we already promoted a gay person on the board of directors. So, we aren't prejudice,"

Is This Always a Bad Thing?

It can be argued that this is not a bad thing because it can reduce prejudice amongst minority groups. (Plant et al, 2009)

Resulting in an increase in the self-esteem of the people that are hired as long as they don't know they were only hired because of this policy. (Unzuet et al, 2010)

But as I've already mentioned this policy can be used to deflect accusation of prejudice. (Dutton & Lake, 1973)

Also, it can result in reverse discrimination were people who harbour negative attitudes openly showing pro-minority behaviours.

At first, this sounds positive but it doesn't decrease prejudice since you aren't changing the behaviour or opinion.

Affirmative Action:

Building upon this further, people are seen as less competent if they're hired under this policy. (Heilman et al, 1992)

This makes sense because you weren't hired because you were good at the job. Instead, you were hired for the sole purpose of meeting a quota.

Also, "Quotas" mean people don't make an effect to fight prejudice in other ways.

As a result, they can just say to people. "We aren't sexist. We met the quotas for having 50% of our board female,"

Then you might find that 50% of females carries less weight when the board votes on matters.

Positive Feedback Bias:

Now, this bias is one of the 'better' bias to have when you consider the other thinking bias humans have.

However, the positive feedback bias is, for example, when teachers mark work less critically and higher if it's from a minority group member. (Harber,

1998)

I know the teachers are probably trying to be nice but it could be harmful because it makes the student think they're better than they are. Meaning they could struggle later in life.

Also, it could be considered patronising.

Finally, this could be self-serving as it helps prove to the person or marker that they're not prejudice.

CHAPTER 27: CATEGORIZATION APPROACHES, INTERGROUP CONTACT AND APOLOGY

Another interesting way to improve group relations is using category-based approaches.

<u>Recategorization:</u>

This is when people of different groups categorise themselves to be part of the same group and attitudes improve (Gartner & Dovidio, 2000)

In my opinion, this is interesting because it shows the entire reason why bad intergroup relations exist is because different groups view themselves are different.

Yet if we get people to think of themselves as members of the same group with common goals then this can improve intergroup relations. (Gaertner et al, 1999)

Nonetheless, this can backfire in high identifiers. For example, Crisp, Stone & Hall (2006) told British students that Britain was joining the United States of Europe and British was an old way of identifying yourself.

Their results showed extremely high levels of ingroup favouritism towards British people.

This effect is understandable as the mutual differentiation model. (Brewer, 1991) shows groups need to be distinctive.

Values-based approaches:

These approaches focus on values. Such as: tolerance, multiculturalism, and egalitarianism. As well as they discourage hateful and competitive attitudes. (Grandale & Eslleman, 2003)

These approaches can defuse negative intergroup relations (Bovidio et al, 1996) And using categories to combat prejudice can work but it can backfire if people feel like they are losing their identity.

Although, identity complexity and multicultural ideology could help. Since it changes the way people think about their ingroup and attaches values to diversity.

I quite like this approach to intergroup relations since I love multiculturalism and I don't see any problems with it.

Also, I support discouraging hateful and competitive attitudes since this is the time I think the world needs to come together and it shouldn't fracture into self-interested shards.

Now we'll going to talk about my favourite method to improving relations.

Intergroup contact:

This is my favourite topic about improving relations because… well you'll see in a moment.

"The Troubles"

For people who don't live in the UK or Republic of Ireland, the Troubles could be oversimplified to say it was a 30-year political conflict that was surrounded by violence on both sides.

And yet this reduction in violence is an inspirational example of intergroup reconciliation. But this wasn't done through contact.

Instead, this was done by dividing up Belfast with "Peace Walls,"

Yet 100s of studies suggest this shouldn't happen.

The Contact Hypothesis:

This proposes under appropriate conditions, contact between different members of social groups can lead to a reduction in intergroup bias. (Allport, 1955; Amire 1969)

In addition, contact works when it's supported by authorities and social norms and when people have equal status, common goals and cooperation.

This is built upon further by Pettigrth and Tropp's (2006) meta-analysis of 515 articles. They found these factors don't have to be present but they help and the factors and people working together matter rather than separately.

Overall, contact requires the opportunity and they want to engage in a meaningful way with the outgroup. As well as meaningful contact is unlikely in situations of pervasive conflict and segmentation.

I think this makes sense because if you get to meet other people that you don't like, and you get know them. Then you find out they're good people and the stereotypes are wrong. This should result in a decrease in prejudice.

Like I know despite the stereotypes the French are great people and Muslims are very kind.

However, I understand there needs to be a want

to decrease prejudice. Like: there is no hope on earth I would decrease my prejudice and disdain for white supremacy. Since I do NOT want to meet a white supremacist so if I met one. I wouldn't be happy and this contact would probably result in an increase in prejudice towards this outgroup.

<u>The Reality:</u>

Although some question the reality of this contact approach as Lee (2003) mentioned there are too many conditions not realistic in situations, people avoid contact find it highly stigmatising.

Also, when groups come into contact, some of this is a negative interaction. This studies like Barlow et al (2012) have found negative contact has a larger impact than positive contact.

Barlow's contact only adds to what I mentioned above.

Personally, I understand this questioning because we do tend to stick together, and we stick to those areas. For instance, if you look at the communities in London. You'll see the different ethnic communities have their clear areas.

Of course, they'll be some white people in the areas dominated by black people and vice versa. But the areas are still pretty clear.

Thankfully, there's a way to overcome this questioning of reality.

Extended Contact Hypothesis:

Wright et al (1997) found indirect forms of contact are very important. For example, you don't have contact with an outgroup, but your friends do.

As always, I was naturally interested in this strange sounding idea, so one way how this works is your friends tell you about the outgroup. Then this results in:

- Reduction in intergroup anxiety (Parlini et al, 2004)
- Changes group norms to make the outgroup acceptance and decrease prejudice. (Wright et al, 1997)
- Inclusion of outgroup in the self. (Cameron et al, 2006)

Imagined Intergroup Contact:

Amazingly enough, even imagining intergroup conflict can help.

"The mental stimulation of social interaction with a member of an outgroup category" (Crisp, Stalthe, Turner & Husnii, 2008)

Mental Imagery:

This works because it elicits similar emotional and motivational responses as the real experience. (Sadds, Bowbjerg, Redd & Cutrne, 1992) as well as it employs similar neurological mechanisms. Such as memory, emotion and motor control. (Farah, 1989; Kossyln, Ganis & Thompson, 2001)

In other words, you can the same benefits as meeting people in real life.

A Verdict on Contact:

Overall, contact is a much-researched technique and it can backfire, sometimes it backfires, sometimes it doesn't.

Whilst, it is sometimes unrealistic. It can be simulated by extended or imagined contact.

Nonetheless, recent metal analysis show direct and indirect contact can work in real life to reduce prejudice. (Lemmer & Wagner, 2015)

Meaning it is a good technique overall.

Intergroup apology:

I have been waiting ages to write this chapter because I'll admit I'm going to get a bit political because the UK Government's bad handling of the COVID-19 pandemic really helps me in this chapter.

But when a group transgresses an apology is often expected, and the purpose of this is to allow the perpetrators and victims groups to reconcile.

In addition, according to Blarz et al (2009), these 10 elements should be present in all governmental apologies but only some of these elements ever are.

Equally, I'm going to only talk about 8 of them.

And yes, this is where I talk about the UK Government because personally, I'm still waiting for the Government to admit they made mistakes in the past 9 months.

According to the Government, they have never made a mistake in the pandemic which is annoying because people make mistakes and that's fine.

The important thing is you need to learn from your mistakes.

The UK Government hasn't done either.

<u>What's Needed in an Apology:</u>

- You need to show remorse.
- The Government needs to accept responsibility.

In the case of the UK Government, it could be as simple as "We're sorry we knew about the new Variant of COVID from late November but we didn't do anything until Mid- December. A few days before Christmas,"

- Admit injustice or wrong
- Acknowledge harm
- Offer reparation- another term for compensation.
- Minimize resistance from own group. Such as "We are better now"
- Praise current system

Personally, I think the UK Government has tried this feature to death because it has kept mentioning how brilliant our Track and Trace system is when it isn't.

Therefore, I think even if the UK Government tried this feature. I doubt it would work.

- Disassociate from the past.

In other words, try and move on from this transgression.

Nonetheless, people tend to feel insulted by apology with reparations but no remorse.

This happened to myself and other cohorts at University during the 2019 and 2020 university strikes since my University offered us a Goodwill payment.

Yet the email was worded in an unremorseful way and they really encouraged us to donate our money to a COVID-19 fund.

Personally, I just thought: *you only want us to stop moaning and you just want us to give us your money back so you don't have to spend as much on the COVID fund.*

Finally, apologies tend to have little impact on forgiveness. (Blake & Philpat, 2010) but they're better than nothing. As well as the public's memory for apologies are poor (Homsey & Wohl, 2013)

CHAPTER 28: COLLECTIVE ACTION

The way of improving group relations, we're going to look at is known as Collective Action and this is an interesting idea, I think because it's not as cut and dry as people would think.

So, some intergroup relationships are marked by inequality, and dealing with it sometimes requires coordinated actions of disadvantaged group members to change intergroup relations.

In addition, this is often taken on behalf of the wider cause of justice and needs of other groups. (Thomas & McGarty, 2009)

But people are most likely to do collective action on behalf of their own group.

Therefore, people can protest (Van Zomeren et al, 2008) and lobby, organised charity events, or volunteer as part of collective action. (Thomas et al, 2008)

Leading us to the question below.

What Motivates Collective Action?

According to Van Zomeren et al (2008), three interrelated variables motivated it.

- High Identify with group
- Perceive injustice
- Perceived efficacy of the group to change its situation.

If we cast our minds back to the Audible Situation, I spoke about earlier in the book. The Author community is taking collective action against Audible because we identify highly with the author group.

Furthermore, we perceive Audible is an injustice because they're hiding returns data and they're stealing money from authors.

Finally, as the Society of Authors, the Alliance of Independent Authors and many other professional organisations are behind the author community in this collective action. There is a perceived efficacy of the group to change its situation.

I really hope we succeed.

Update in late January 2020, we did succeed!

Collective Action Vs Prejudice Reduction:

Nonetheless, Dixon, Levine, Reciler & Durrhein (2012) argue that prejudice reduction by itself isn't an effective way to end discrimination and disadvantage.

Also, it may end up suppressing the minority group's willingness to take action.

Although, the study that the idea of collective action was based off is problematic because there's very little research to support collective action results in social change.

For example, Louis (2009) and Van Zomeren (2005) found there was little theory on when and how collective action should work. But Louis (2009) could be a useful study in explaining this theory.

Also, collective action can be threatening to majorities so it can backfire.

This can be seen with the Black Lives Matter Movement since I saw a few news reports of people in the UK and USA were people weren't racism before the Movement (well they say that) but seeing the mass of protesters outside their homes and riots and looting in the street, made them feel threatened. Hence, their support dramatically drops for the Movement.

Personally, I still support the Black Lives

Movement because it was the minority that looted and all these people want is for their lives to matter as much as white people.

Plus, over Christmas 2020 there was another murder of a Black man by a white police officer when this man was only delivering Christmas money to his friend.

So, clearly there is still work to be done but hopefully things will improve over time.

Finally, prejudice majorities are unlikely to take action on behalf of minorities or to support their efforts.

Again, this makes sense, because why would you stick your neck out for an outgroup?

Conclusion:

Overall, many techniques are shown to help reduce prejudice and they may have helped reduce group-based prejudice.

However, it can be argued that this still hasn't helped reduce economic inequality within nations. This has increased and there is recent evidence of increases in prejudice

PART FOUR: SOCIAL INFLUENCE

CHAPTER 29: SOCIAL INFLUENCE

We are all influenced by others and social influence is the effects that other people can have on our thoughts, feelings and behaviour.

Social influence can be divided into a few types including conformity, obedience as well as compliance and acceptance.

In addition, conformity can be good, bad or inconsequential. An example of good conformity is not pushing in a queue at a supermarket.

Whereas compliance can change behaviour but not belief as well as acceptance is when you change your behaviour and belief.

For example, I comply with the social norm of going to lectures at university but my belief is that sometimes just doing the reading and looking at the slides is more than enough.

Furthermore, Markus and Kitayara (1991) proposed that conformity is the 'social glue' that holds a society together.

Additionally, radicalisation is a special type of social influence where people are encouraged to strike out at a society that is deemed to be fundamentally wrong. (Ryan, 2007)

Key Studies:

Before we dive into the psychology and the theory of social influence and how it affects our behaviour. We need to learn several vital studies.

Sheriff (1935, 1937)

Sheriff was interested in the emergence of social norms.

Therefore, in his experiment he got participants to sit in a dark room and they had to observe a light. This led to the autokinetic effect- where you look at the light for a long time and you think it moves when it doesn't; then the light suddenly disappears.

Afterwards, the participant on their own is asked to estimate how much the light moved. Later, they do it again but are given two estimates from other participants.

The results show that when other answers were given, they convergent over time. Equalling a new social judgement norm. This norm persists overtime when asked to rate it again, you continue the norm.

The reasons for these findings is the ambiguous stimulus; the light; gave the participants an internal frame of reference. This was combined with the differential judgement of others to create another frame of reference. Overall, with both frames of reference in mind, it was easier to give a value of movement. This created a norm in the process.

For example, if I thought 4cm but someone else said 6cm then I would have probably said 5cm of movement. Subsequently, over time as more and more answers got said a norm would develop as the difference between 5cm and 6cm is nothing in terms of social norms.

Asch (1951, 1952, 1956)

In this study, the participant was seated 6th in a row of 7 people and they were presented with a diagram with a standard line to compare to 3 comparison lines. The participant needed to choose which comparison line matches the standard.

The experiment had three trials so in trial 1 everyone before the participant agreed on the same line. This was the correct one. For trial 2, everyone agreed on the correct line, but on trial 3 all confederates chose the wrong line.

Overall, the results showed that the control group; were everyone gave their answers individually; 99% of them chose the correct line. Compared to only 63% of the experimental group.

This is a brilliant quote from Asch (1955) because he summarises the results perfectly as the young people knew that the line was wrong but they choose it anyway.

'well-meaning young people are willing to call white black' (Asch, 1955)

Although, these findings are very interesting because in this situation there is no obvious pressure to comply, so it's odd that people do comply.

CHAPTER 30: MILGRAM (1965, 1975)

Milgram's study must be one of the most famous psychology case studies because of how impressive and unethical it is.

This study wanted to examine the effects of punishment on learning, at least this is what the participants were told. In reality, the study was examining the effects of conformity.

Therefore, in the study, the participant was to teach another person a series of paired words and then test their memory, and if the participant got the words wrong then they would be punished with an electrical shock. The learner is a confederate trained on how to respond and the response that the participant heard were all recordings.

Additionally, the shocks ranged from a slight shock of 15 volts to 450-volts labelled XXX and the teacher was asked to deliver a higher level of shock each time the learner makes a mistake.

<u>The Study's Procedure:</u>

Firstly, the teacher; the participant; takes a mild electrical shock to know what it's like then they see the learner being strapped to a chair and electrodes attached to their wrists.

Subsequently, the teacher would continue to shock the confederate each time they got an answer wrong, as well as each time the participant wanted to stop shocking the confederate. They would be urged on by the researcher.

Interestingly, before the experiment began 110 experts said what they expected to happen in the experiment. These experts predicted that only 10% of people would exceed 110 volts and nobody would reach the 450 volts.

However, in reality, over 50% of people reach the 450-volt mark, but obedience decreased as shocks increased, as well as 63% of teachers went up and beyond the 450-volts.

The reasons why the researchers got these results will be explored throughout this chapter.

<u>Milgram's Other Studies:</u>

Milgram conducted another 18 experiments with very similar results across all studies. He found that there was no difference in conformity for men and women as well as there were only a few cross-cultural differences.

These studies tell us that attitudes fail to determine behaviour when external influences override them.

The Stanford Prison Experiment:

This is another famous psychology experiment that is… beyond unethical.

The Standard Prison Experiment happened in the summer of 1971; and whilst there are some modern questions about its findings; it stills shows the power of titles and social influence.

In the experiment, 24 participants were assigned to be prisoners or guards. The people who were prisoners were arrested, cuffed and taken to prison as well as they were processed like real prisoners.

In addition, the prison guards were dressed in a Khaki and wore sunglasses to dehumanise the guards.

On the first night, a prisoner rebellion sparked authoritative guard behaviour. Leading to the prisoners to be harassed and degraded.

In fact, this degradation got bad enough that the experiment had to stop after 6 days compared to the originally planned 14 days.

Power of Situation:

Both Milgram and the Stanford Prison Experiment argue about the power of the situation as some situations are evil. Leading to moral judgement to be suspended.

- 'The Lucifer Effect'- this is where a person crosses the line between good and bad and does an evil act.
- 'the banality of evil'. This is where a person doesn't believe they are committing evil instead they are doing a behaviour that society has normalised. (Hannah Arendt, 1963)

However, Adderly Eichmann was responsible for the Nazi 'final situation' and he willingly chose to do this act.

Therefore, it's not always about the situation as People often choose to be in a certain position (Blass, 1991).

Nonetheless, these studies were designed to allow evil to flourish and they were commanded by people in leadership roles who were given instructions to be 'evil'. Hence, it's possible that these studies lack ecological validity; were the experiment reflects the real world; as in the real world, nobody or only a few people are told to be evil. This questions the validity of the findings.

CHAPTER 31: WHY PEOPLE CONFORM?

Individual/Tasks Factor:

People are more likely to conform when the task they're doing is difficult so they conform as a way to get help, as well as people, conform when they feel uncomfortable and insecure.

Group:

Groups are extremely powerful things and they can make us do even more powerful things. Hence, why there's a whole chapter dedicated to groups- but these are the group factors that can cause conformity.

Asch (1955) found that groups of 3-5 people elicit greater conformity than groups of 1-2, yet after 5 people it makes no difference. This demonstrates how the group size can increase conformity rates.

Unanimity- Asch (1955) found if someone

dissents then conformity only happens about 25% of the time. Hence, demonstrating how conformity can decrease as a result of deviants or people who don't conform.

Lastly, Milgram (1974) found that 'blue-collar' workers were most influenced by the 'professor'. Hence, showing the power of status in terms of conformity.

Contextual Factors:

As demonstrated in one of Milgram's studies they found that the further the authority figure was from the participant. The more obedience dropped.

This can be in terms of physical proximity like distance in metres or emotional proximity. Such as: being able to hear or see them.

This immediacy effect could possibly have something to do with us being closer to the learner. Allowing us to become more aware of their humanity and we are more likely to empathise with them.

Linking to the concept of dehumanisation; were seeing groups as less than human; allows people to justify atrocities against them. As shown in the Stanford Prison Experiment.

The legitimacy of the authority figure is important as well as people are sensitive to the legitimacy of the figure and they use this to determine if conformity is right or not.

Group Related Factors:

As demonstrated in another version of Milgram's classic study. He found that peer pressure is an important predictor of compliance, because when two participants were in the room and they both refused to go past a certain voltage point. Compliance dropped to as low as 10% Whereas two obedient peers raised compliance with 92.5%

Overall, people use peers to judge the legitimacy and appropriate course of action.

Generally, groups who are unanimous and closely bound together are difficult to resist.

One explanation for this is that if the member's dissent then they risk the group's disapproval and social disapproval is a very powerful thing.

However, if someone has already vocalised a response then the pressure of the group can rarely change their mind. (Deutsch and Gerard, 1955)

This phenomenon is more than stubbornness because if a person goes against or reverses a decision then this can cause them to lose face, so they will often stick to their decision even if they lose out.

The similarity attraction hypothesis is linked to

social influence as when people are in a setting with like-minded others (Abrams, Wetherdell, Cockhrane et al, 1990) and when a person has friends in the group (Thibaut and Stockland, 1956) conformity increases.

People can conform for two reasons:

- Normative influence- the social influence that arises from the need to gain social approval from others.

Basically, 'you go along with the crowd' to meet people's positive expectations.

Interestingly with a normative influence attempt, people are more likely to disagree with the group, but they suppress their disagreement in order to be liked.

- Informational influence- the social influence that comes from the desire to be correct so they can accept information from others.

Particularly happens in an ambiguous social setting.

Referent Information Influence:

This is when we are socially influenced to conform to a group because we are members and adherence to group norms defines us as a member.

For example, as a member of my university's baking society, I always adhere to the norms of being social and having fun because in order to be a part of the group I need to follow these norms.

Who is influenced?

Many social psychologists argue that there are personality types or characteristics that make people more likely to be influenced.

However, there is no research to support these claims and there are a lot of contradictory or weak findings. (Mischel, 1969)

Equally, the research is very mixed and inconclusive about gender differences towards conformity as some research suggests that women are susceptible to influence.

However, Milgram (1974) and Eagly (1987) and other studies haven't found such claims.

However, experimental design can be important as these tasks can be more familiar to men. Leading women to be less sure and a lower conformity rating.

Minority Influence:

After looking at the reasons why people conform and how people are affected by social influence. In this last section, we will be focusing on how minority groups can influence people. As a result, this is difficult to do and this is how most social movements start off, as a minority. The process of minority groups gaining influence is called innovation.

Interestingly, minority influence wasn't investigated until the 1960s after the women's rights movement but during the black right movements by Moscovici.

Consequently, Moscovici (1976) found that the influence of minorities can't be accounted for by the same principles that explain majority influence.

As a result, there are fewer people in these minority group, they have less control and they have less access to information.

Therefore, he argued that the minority's impact lies in their own behavioural style because their behaviour needs to be clear, consistent over time (diachronic consistency and stable over time.

<u>Synchronic Consistency:</u>

This type of consistency states that minority group members all need to be on the same page. Otherwise, they won't be as effective.

Moreover, minority groups are less likely to be influenced by normative influence because there is no normality pressure from the majority.

On the other hand, most influence occurs on a more private level and being in the minority groups evokes a validation process, so the person feels like their opinions are right.

Lastly, as the participant thinks more closely about issues. The participants become more likely to be privately influenced However, majority pressure may prevent this from being shown publicly.

CHAPTER 32: CONTROVERSIES OF THE EXPERIMENTS

A few chapters ago, we spoke about a number of experiments that suggest the power of the situation. Personally, I love those studies despite their extremely unethical procedure.

However, in this chapter, I'm going to talk about some more questionable aspects of the research.

When I was taught this at university, I was very interested in this topic since no one talks about it.

What Was Reported Vs What Happened:

In all honesty, the quotes will shout more than I will but Nicholson (2011) found some very interesting results.

Firstly, in Milgram (1964) "all participants were told that the victim has not received dangerous electric shocks"

In reality, after the experiment, they weren't told this straight away, as supported by participants who said: "I was pretty well shook up for a few days after the experiment. It would have helped if I had been told the facts shortly after"; "I seriously question the wisdom and ethics of not completely dehoaxing each subject immediately after the session" and "I actually checked the death notices in the New Haven Register for at least two weeks after the experiment…"

I think this is appalling because just imagine checking to see if you had killed anyone for two weeks after your experiment.

<u>Intense Distress:</u>

Another interesting point was Milgram (1965/1972) admitted they caused intense distress, but they insisted that post-experiment screening revealed no lasting harm.

Yet again, Nicholson (2011) found participants said differently.

For example:

- "I was…. just completely depressed for a while"
- "By coincidence, a fellow employee had taken part in the same experiment… Later we compared notes… during one of our discussions I… said things I normally never

would say… I used some vulgar words and shortly thereafter because of other conditions I lost my job"

- "since taking part in the experiment I have suffered a mild heart attack…. I feel it is imperative you make certain that any prospective participant get a clean bill of health"

Again, I think this is disgusting that one experiment had such devastating consequences.

On the other hand, I am extremely glad we have the measures we have in now and the ethical guidelines.

Off-Script:

This point I found weird and comical since Griffs & Whitehead (2015) found the experimenters in the Milgram study went off-script.

Due to the four prompts were never meant to be coercive techniques. They were meant to be stopping points of the experiment.

Meaning the funny part of the experiment was the only reason why the study got the results it did was because of these coercive techniques.

Additional Research Problems:

Another problem with these studies as Carnahan & McFarland (2007) found fewer people would volunteer for a 'psychological study of prison life' compared to a 'psychological study'.

Therefore, you get a very bias sample since the people that signed up for the study were more aggressive, more narcissistic, authoritarian, machiavellian, (the willingness to manipulate others for personal gain) Social Dominance Oriented and less altruistic as well as empathic.

Overall, this makes for a very poor research sample because all these participants were not the average person.

Therefore, this only adds to the debate surrounding the generalisability of the findings.

Lack of Ecological Validity:

Whilst, we're all pointing out the problems with these major studies. We must add that the studies were carefully created to allow 'evil' to flourish and in the real world, it could be more difficult for evil to flourish. Due to several confounding variables.

Afterwards, the situations were maintained as well as worsened by individual behaviour. This can be clearly seen in the Stanford Prison Experiment where the guards did what they did because the researchers gave them no guidance.

As supported by these instructions by Zimbardo to the guards at the beginning of the experiment:

"We can create in the prisoners feelings of boredom, a sense of fear to some degree, we can create a notion of arbitrariness that their life is totally controlled by us, by the system, you, me… They'll have no freedom of action, they can do nothing, or say nothing that we don't permit. We're going to take away their individuality in various ways."

One important thing to note about these vague instructions is that these are as detailed as the instructions during the holocaust. This made the guards need to be more creative and devise torture methods.

This feeds into the idea that it is the situation and people that interact to create good and evil. (Haslam & Reicher, 2007, Review) Since the prison situation didn't make evil, and the guards alone weren't evil before they interacted with the situation.

Two major factors play additional roles in the creation of evil because identification plays an important role (Levine & Crowther, 2008; Reicher & Haslam, 2006) as does ideology. For example, ideologies about dominance and equality. (Sidanius et al., 2003).

As a result, people who highly identify with the role of guard and has high ideologies around dominating people. These people are likely to be more 'evil' when interacting with the situation.

Are Groups Always More Risky?

I know the past few chapters have been depressing reads that show the downsides of human behaviour and social groups.

But I want to stress social groups aren't always riskier than being alone.

For example, Abrams, Hopthrow, Hulbert and Frings (2006) studied risk orientation in groups compared to people alone and after consuming alcohol vs a placebo.

Their results showed when people were alone, people found riskier choices more attractive. This was eliminated when in groups.

PART FIVE:
PERSUASION

CHAPTER 33: PERSUASION

Persuasion is about Influencing people and it is the process by which a message changes a person's behaviour and attitudes. Persuasion has benefits and negatives as well.

In addition, Howland, Janis and Kelley (1953) found four steps in persuasion. You need to get the target's attention; you need to offer compensation for this cost to their attention; this is your offer; they need to accept your offer and you need to retain their attention.

Additionally, they found that persuasion can have four outcomes. Persuasion should change someone's opinion, perception, emotion or actions.

Over the next three sections, we'll be looking at the most important features of a persuasion attempt that people need to get right in order to be successful in their persuasion.

These features are The Source, The Message and The Method.

Source:

The source of a persuasion attempt is usually the person persuading you.

Attractiveness:

In addition, being attractive can be very helpful in persuasion attempts because people imagine themselves being the model and having healthy attractive skin.

Additionally, the more attractive the person the more likely the persuasion attempt has of succeeding, as well as attempts are most successful when an attractive and emotive person is the source.

In their experiment, Eagly and Chaiken (1975) had attractive and unattractive people try to get students to sign a petition. The results showed that the attractive people had a sign-up rate of 41% but the unattractive students only had a 32% success rate.

Lastly, Kutzner, Fielder and Freytag (2010) demonstrated people anticipated success of persuasion attempts based on the attractiveness of the persuader.

Similarity:

Similarity or familiarity is persuasive because those we are similar to, we tend to like more.

For example, I am more likely to like a university student, or I am more a lot more likely to like other authors because both groups are similar to me.

Petty, Cacioppo and Goldman (1981) had a student give an evaluation of a speech and it was said that this speech was written by a person from this or another university. The results showed that people liked the speech more if it was from their university.

Therefore, showing that similarity is important as when people think you are similar to themselves, they find you more persuasive.

Other Important Features:

Here are some other factors to consider as these are important for persuasion success:

- If we think someone has an ulterior motive or is trying to manipulate us then the persuasion can fail. (Wolster and Festinger, 1962)
- Fragle and Heath (2004) repeated exposure to a message can cause the creditability of the source to increase and this increases the likelihood of persuasion.

- The sleeper effect is when a message isn't persuasive at first but over time as the typically low creditability speaker is forgotten the message becomes persuasive.

Furthermore, when people are more likeable they tend to be more persuasive. This links into the similarity concept as people that are similarity to us are seen as more qualified than dissimilar people, and a person is even more persuasive if the source is credible and trustworthy.

Therefore, celebrities can be persuasive because they tend to be extremely well-liked and attractive. This adds to their persuasive power.

However, once celebrities become uncredited, they are no longer persuasive, so companies usually drop them in an effort to save their brand.

Finally, it's important to remember that the message is still very important and the source and the message still need to work together in order to maximise chances of being persuasive.

CHAPTER 34: THE MESSAGE

The message is the entire point of the persuasion attempt because the persuader is trying to persuade you as the target to do something. Like: don't smoke, do this new diet and more.

Overall, long messages are more effective if they're strong but long messages are less effective when the message or argument is weak. (Petty and Cacippo, 1984) as well as messages need to be consistent with the attitude of the target- or the message cannot be too far from the target's original attitude.

For an argument to be strong it needs to include facts and figures.

For instance, Liberman and Chaiken (1992) found that coffee drinkers are more likely to reject an argument linking caffeine consumption with ill health than the non-coffee drinkers.

On a personal note, as a coffee drinker myself, I agree with the findings and whilst I know that coffee is bad for you. I take the road that says everything is bad for you in excess so I limit myself to two cups of coffee a day. Unless if I'm going out for a meal or to Wetherspoons because they have unlimited coffee for £1.35.

Repetition:

Unsurprisingly, when it comes to the message repetition is very important because we're more likely to be persuaded by something we're seen repeatedly.

One example is that in the business world, there's an idea that you need to see something about seven times before you buy it, as well as Tellis (1987) found that advertisements are most effective when people see them about 2-3 times a week.

Although, advertisements can 'wear out' if they are shown too often.

I know this from personal experience because when most adverts are shown on television. I show indifference towards them because I have seen them so many times.

Finally, advertising is most effective when people respond positively and have familiarity with the product. (Campbell and Keller, 2003)

Fear arousal:

Getting people scared can be a very powerful thing. This is probably why politicians and others use it often.

Overall, fear arousal can work most of the time (Leventwal, Watts and Pagano, 1967) because you make people feel bad. Such as the stopping smoking campaign in the UK.

However, Aronson (1997) argued that fear arousal sometimes doesn't work because people can engage with denial behaviour, as well as a moderate fear level is best.

But denial can be avoided when a proper solution is presented. (Devos-Combey and Salovey, 2002)

For instance, an advert that says smoking will kill you isn't likely to be effective because people will be in denial as this promotes a lot of fear.

To solve this problem a better advert would be smoking will kill you so join The Smokers Club today to quit smoking forever and live a long life!

Factual versus Emotional Messages:

Factual and emotional messages can both be highly effective but educated people and people those attitudes were formed by facts tend to be persuaded by the factual message. Whereas the people who had their attitudes and opinions formed with emotion tend to be persuaded by emotive messages more.

CHAPTER 35: THE METHOD AND MODELS OF PERSUASION

The method is vital in a persuasion attempt because if you don't deliver your message in an effective way then your persuasion attempt will fail.

One method of delivering the message is to form a two-sided message. This is when the persuader acknowledges both sides of the argument and this is particularly useful for people who are aware of both sides of the argument. (Jones and Breham, 1970)

Personally, these types of messages are a lot more likely to work on me because I love balance and balanced opinions. As quite often when I see someone only focusing on one side of the argument. Instead of focusing on their message, I focus on trying to understand the other side.

Order:

If you want to be successful in persuasion getting the order right in your argument is vital because the information that is presented first tends to be most persuasive (Asch, 1946) and people tend to side more with arguments they have heard first. (Miller and Campbell, 1959)

In addition, if people are presented with information then a week later they get a new piece of information. This new piece will be more persuasive as people forget the first piece of information.

Overall, throughout this section, we will explore what factors are needed in order to make the information you hear first or the information you hear later more persuasive.

This links to the primacy and recency effect.

Primacy and Recency Effects:

The primacy effect is the idea that ideas and information that you hear first are the most important.

Whereas the recency effect is the idea that the information you hear towards the end of an argument is the most persuasive. Especially, during a long argument.

Channel:

The way the message is presented is very important as Television is effective for persuasion but when the information is more complex written channels are better. (Chaiken and Eagly, 1976)

Gender:

Personally, I'm not a fan of this research but research shows that women are more susceptible to persuasion especially in face to face persuasion attempts as women are more cooperation focused.

However, the research is likely to be skewed as male experimenters designed the experiments using male topics. Meaning that the women were disadvantaged in these experiments.

Age:

Personally, I find age to be an interesting topic to investigate because I look at some groups and I'm amazed at how easy they are to persuade than I look at others and think how hard they are to persuade.

The research shown that late adolescents and young adults are more susceptible as attitudes are less stable, as well as they are less resistant to authority.

The reason is these findings is because these years are seen as the 'impressionable years' and are easy to influence (Jears, 1986) and Fung and Catst

Carstensen (2003) found that the message content matters as older adults preferred more meaningful messages whereas the young adult people didn't.

Personality:

Overall, these results are complicated as there are many factors involved.

One example of how personality can impact persuasion is people's need for cognition. This is how much enjoyment people get from thinking and if people get a lot of enjoyment from thinking then they are more likely to be persuaded.

In my opinion, I love thinking and I like to work through problems so I have a high Need for Cognition.

Whereas, Need For Cognitive Closure is where people are cognitively close-minded and want to quick or certain answers to questions. These people are less susceptible to persuasion as they're closed-minded and make up their minds quickly.

Mood:

For mood, good feeling messages are more persuasive as they make people feel good as they increase positive feeling and thinking which in turns increases impulsive decision making. (Bodenhausen, 1993)

Models of Persuasion:

The Elaboration Likelihood Model:

The elaboration Likelihood model is a model that states that people's success for their persuasion attempt is dependent on whether people are willing to elaborate or think about the argument.

It argues that people depend on their cognitive effort level and they focus on different features of a persuasive argument. (Petty and Cacioppo, 1986)

For example, people focus on the central cues. Which are the features of an argument.

However, you can be persuaded by peripheral cues as well. These are features of a message that don't require a lot of mental considerations.

The model's two roots to persuasion states then if a group has low motivation then they use peripheral cues to be persuasive. Whereas if a group has high motivation then you need to focus on core cues in order to persuade them.

Heuristic System Model.

This model is like the last one.

It argues that people take two approaches to the message:

- Heuristic- where people use a mental shortcut to deal with the information as dealing with a lot of detailed information is just too much. (Chaiken, 1987)
- System thinking- when people actively progress and engage the information in front of them.

Factors Determining Route:

The following factors determine which route is taken when thinking about a persuasive message:

- Ability to focus- people who are distracted aren't likely to focus on the core cues as they require more energy. Thus, they take the peripheral route.
- Motivation- people need to be motivated or interested so they can focus on the central cue routes.
- Mood- being in a sad mood is when people typically tend to take the heuristic route. (Bohner, Chaiken and Hungadu, 1994)

CHAPTER 36: PERSUASION TECHNIQUES AND WHEN PERSUASION DOESN'T WORK

Techniques:

There are a lot of great persuasive techniques that people can use and these techniques include the lowball tactic. This is where you add hidden costs once the target has already committed to the purchase as well as research shows once committed, people don't tend to change their minds.

Another persuasion technique is the That's not all technique. This is where persuaders offer people one product then a little while later they throw some more bonuses to get the target to reciprocate.

Furthermore, when this technique is used more people tend to be persuaded by this influence. (Burger, 1986)

This is where you get people to like you before

ask for the persuasive attempt. (Smith, Pruitt and Carnevate, 1982) and this can be very effective but this can backfire if it's obvious as if you're too nice people will become suspicious.

In addition, the reciprocity principle where you do them a favour, for a favour can be very effective.

Some other techniques include:

- Face in the floor technique- where you make a very large easy to refuse offer before making a smaller more realistic offer. (Cialdini, 1984) it works because as you've made a concession the target feels obliged to make their own concession as well.
- Foot in the door- ask something small then ask for something bigger. Since a person is already committed they are more likely to grant the large request. Charities make very good use of this persuasion technique.
- The scarcity technique is effective as people believe that it's rare. As demonstrated in Warchel, Lee and Adevole (1975) who gave participants a chocolate chip cookie and asked them to rate it. The conditions that they took the cookies from cookie jars with 2 cookies or 10 cookies in it. The results showed that participants rated the cookies as desirable when taking from the cookie jar with only 2 cookies in it. This was because that cookie jar made the cookies seem rarer.

Why Persuasion Doesn't Always Work:

Thankfully, persuasion doesn't always work as if it did we would constantly be buying everything and our political attitudes would constantly be shifting.

Persuasion doesn't work for a number of reasons include:

- Reactance- this is where people react strongly against blatant or persistent influence attempts. Then they can get increasingly annoyed and react. Usually by adopting a completely different attitude. (Brehn, 1966) and (Rhodewalt and Davison, 1983)
- Forewarning- people have time to have to prepare counterarguments or you aren't even likely to enter a persuasion attempt. Some research suggests that when people are forewarned about the persuasion attempt it tends to fail because the forewarning activates several cognitive functions that we are important for persuasion. (Johnson, 1994) and (Cialdini and Petty, 1979)
- Counterarguing- people can actively resist persuasion attempts by addressing and arguing against attitude cogent argument directly.
- Attitudes invocation- presenting a weak, attitude consistent argument before a stronger persuasive helps them to resist the message.

This considering 'inoculates them' because they can create more counterarguments.

- Selective avoidance- people tend to filter out information that is opposing their attitude
- Attitude polarisation- people tend to evaluate mixed information in a way that strengthens attitudes.
- Hostile media bias- people tend to view counter attitudinal media as biased and untrustworthy. (Vallone et al, 1985) yet the Sleeper Effect can fix this problem.

PART SIX: AGRESSION AND CULTURAL PSYCHOLOGY TOPICS

CHAPTER 37: AGRESSION, WHAT CAUSES AGRESSION AND AGRESSION IN SPORT GAMES

Aggression is a very interesting topic because aggression is a part of life, but I'm interested in the why.

Why is aggression a part of humanity and other animals?

Let's begin our exploration…

What is Aggression?

Aggression is a verbal behaviour or physical behaviour that is intended to hurt someone.

This hurt can be:

- Physical
- Social
- Emotional

- Cultural

Two Schools of Thought:

When it comes to questioning whether or not humanity is innately aggressive or gentle. There are two schools of thought.

The first school of thought is John- Jacques Roussan (1754) that proposes that human nature is basically gentle and it is agriculture, technology and urbanisation that fuels violence.

Secondly, you have Thomas Hobbs (1651) that proposes human nature is basically vicious and it is curbed by modern society.

Personally, I believe in Hobbs more because if you think of our history when we need to be aggressive to defend ourselves and to hunt. It's a logical next step to assume that our aggression has been lessened or curbed by our modern societies not needing us to hunt as well.

Evolutionary Perspective:

From an evolutionary perspective, we can expect within species aggression to be common amongst territorial and social species.

In addition, humanity is both a territorial and social species as we defend our territories fiercely; countries; and we have a fundamental need to affiliate.

Gomex et al (2016) found this recently.

History and Aggression:

As I previously mentioned society has potentially curved our aggression as Pinke (2011) argues we are in the least violent period in our history or prehistory through new social norms and civilising behaviour.

This argument has a lot of support.

Empathy and Aggression:

When you first read the subtitle, you probably thought or assumed that people with great amounts of empathy would be very non-aggressive.

Especially, as Pinke (2011) argues we are evolved not only to be aggressive but to have empathy, as well as our civilisation, is getting better at fostering the prosocial side of our nature.

Overall, the general behavioural trends support this idea.

However, across 100 studies, empathic people are only very weakly less aggressive.

In addition, empathy only explains 1.5% of all cases of non-aggressive behaviour. (Vuchan et al, 2014)

This seems relatively universal across all cultures so this could be hard-wired as people are emotionally and automatically averse to doing physical harm.

Source: Crushman et al (2012) and Greene et al (2001)

What Causes Aggression?

Biological Causes:

As discussed in Biological Psychology, our biology has a massive impact on our behaviour, but how does our biology cause aggression?

In early research on aggression, Freud believed that aggression was inherited whereas Thanatos believed that aggression was a death instinct born out of frustration.

On the other hand, a more recent theory is Lorenz (1976) that proposes that aggression is biologically adaptive energy that builds up and eventually needs to be released.

This idea combines ideas from Freud and Darwin, and it is a similar conclusion to Hobbs. Proposing that aggression is inevitable.

In my opinion, this is an interesting idea because it gives some scientific backing to the idea of an aggressive outburst.

Genetics:

I strongly believe that genetics must be involved in aggression because a lot of behaviour can be influenced by various genes.

Twin Studies:

In the aggression research involving genetics, twin studies are used. These are studies that compare twins and you can use them for genetic research as they share a lot more genetic material compared to non-twins.

For example, Tellegen et al (1988) found that if identical twins reported higher levels of aggression so did the other, but this wasn't true for non-identical twins.

Problem With Twin Studies:

Unfortunately, there are a few problems with twin studies.

For example, Environmental similarity, Ramirez (2003) this is a problem were the twins studied didn't share the same environments growing up. Meaning that it could be these different environmental influences that caused the aggression and not the genetics.

Another problem is that aggression that is created in a laboratory setting is different from the aggression created in the real world. (Mils and Carey, 1997)

The Warrior Gene:

According to this concept, in humans, there is the MAOA-X chromosome (Gibbons, 2004) and this gene is responsible for our aggression.

This gene is linked to low serotonin levels and serotonin is needed for emotion regulation.

Please see Biological Psychology for more information.

Additionally, the Warrior Gene concept was used to get Tennessee killer Bradley Waldroup off the death sentence. (Barber, 2010)

However, there is no warrior gene because it is widely believed and I certainly support this idea, but the MAOA gene may interact with an environmental trigger to produce aggression and psychopath. (Caspi et al, 2002; Guo et al, 2008) as well as only 34% of white people have the warrior gene.

Therefore, if the warrior gene idea was true then why can the other 66% of white people be aggressive?

In truth, the warrior gene was created to be a racist slur to explain higher violent offending rates among New Zealand Maori people (Lea et al, 2005) without any supporting evidence (Merrian and

Lameron, 2007)

<u>Warrior Mice:</u>

This last example of genetics I love because this example is brilliant.

As a result, Lagerspetz (1979) bred a race of warrior mice and pacifist mice after 26 generations.

The results showed a race of mice that you couldn't go near and another race of mice that you couldn't provoke.

Another example is Balyer's Russian Silver Fox experiment from 1959 were researchers in Siberia bred from wild foxes, picking the tamest ones to breed from.

This experiment was done in secrecy from the USSR as the Union wasn't interested in biological bases.

The experiment resulted in 3 classes of wolves.

Class 3 foxes-wild wolves that if you should fear towards them. They would bite you.

Class 2- you could pet these wolves, but you couldn't call them friends.

Finally, you have Class 1 wolves. These wolves are very friendly, and they actively seek you out to affiliate.

Overall, this demonstrates that genetics must have something to do with aggression- due to if aggression had nothing to do with genetics then these results would be impossible.

Neuroanatomical:

This line of thinking is consistent with the idea that aggression is hard-wired, instinctive and that parts of our brain are responsible for aggressive tendencies. Such as the amygdala.

One example of this is when Delgado's (1967) found that you can remote control macaques because he implanted an electrode into the amygdala of the macaques. Resulting in it stopped the macaques from being aggressive.

However, he found that if you give other macaques the button that controlled the electrodes then they would learn to control the others.

Overall, there's a lot of research that links the amygdala to aggression.

Neurochemical:

For more information on how neurochemicals work, please check out Biological Psychology.

Some evidence shows testosterone facilitates

aggression.

A bit of this evidence is that chronically high testosterone individuals may be more aggressive and report feeling more restless, as well as they, are more likely to be in prison for an unprovoked violent crime.

Although, these findings are what is known as null experiment findings. This means that the results aren't very significant so testosterone may have very little effect on aggression.

Another neurochemical that might impact aggression is serotonin as it seems to suppress aggression. (Berman et al, 2000) and serotonin is low in depressed people as well as people from low socioeconomic backgrounds.

On the other hand, it has been called into question recently as there isn't a clear relationship between serotonin levels and aggression.

Alcohol:

When it comes to aggression and alcohol, it is preferred by people who are violent when sober and these people are more likely to be aggressive when intoxicated.

Unsurprisingly, alcohol is found in the bloodstream of the offender in 50% rapes and violent crimes, as well as in the bloodstream of victims and /or offenders in 65% of murders.

Alcohol increases the likelihood of aggressive behaviour because it reduces self-awareness and the ability to consider consequences. Resulting in the person being less resistant to the aggressive impulse.

Nonetheless, alcohol and aggression are not clear cut because of a few factors.

For example, alcohol is a drug, yet a fake 'alcohol' produces a powerful placebo effect. (Bergue et al, 2009)

This is partly because of alcohol-related expectancies. This links back to the effects of alcohol to become self-fulfilling as explained earlier.

Biological Conclusion:

In conclusion, it seems that Hobbs is basically right.

There is some indication that human beings are more innately aggressive than most other animals.

Possibly due to our social as well as territorial existence.

Culture of Honour:

To demonstrate the effect that a culture of honour can have on aggression Cohen and Nisbett (1997) conducted a field experiment.

The experiment found that in herding societies people need to protect livestock and these societies tend to have insufficient laws, so you need to be aggressive to earn a reputation and commit to honour.

This idea supports aggression as in the south of the USA.

Frustration- Aggression Hypothesis:

Within social psychology, there is a theory that aggression is formed from frustration.

In this theory, frustration is defined as the blocking of a goal. This increases when there is high motivation to achieve a goal when we expect to achieve the goal and when the goal is completely blocked from us.

Dullard (1939) "frustration always leads to some form of aggression."

Nevertheless, this theory is wrong.

Revised version:

In an effort to revise the theory, Buenstein and Worschel (1962) set up an experiment were the experimental groups wanted to win a prize for teamwork but a confederate kept making them loose.

There were 2 conditions in the experiment. Condition 1 was that the confederate's hearing aid wasn't working so his behaviour wasn't his fault, but in condition 2 he wasn't paying attention so he could control his behaviour.

Results showed when the frustrating person couldn't control the behaviour. This leads to irritation or anger, not aggression.

Aggression can be considered a cognitive script because we learn about aggression through schemas and observational learning.

Berkowitz (1978;1989) frustration leads to anger.

It is this anger that is likely to lead to aggression when cues in the environment remind people about aggressive behaviour.

Social Learning Theory:

As mentioned in Chapter 3, social learning theory or Social Cognitive Theory is where we learn by watching others, and we can apply the theory to aggression.

As a result, aggression is rewarding for the person, so this reinforces the aggressive behaviour. Yet merely watching others being rewarded can influence behaviour.

For example, the bobo doll study mentioned in chapter 3 demonstrates this fact,

Aggression is most likely to occur when we're aroused, and it seems safe and rewarding to be aggressive.

Aggression and Sport games:

I think a lot of people can agree that aggression and sports games go hand in hand as Sarasangi et al (2005) show that Cardiff hospital admissions increase after games at the Millennium stadium. This is especially true after the home team wins.

As a result, there are a lot of different theories that can explain the violence after sports games.

On the whole, research has found that winning makes home team fans feel more aggressive.

As rather than their happiness, this was correlated with their intention of drinking to celebrate and a person's belief about alcohol becomes self-fulling as well.

For example, if you believed that alcohol would make you violent then you are likely to become more violent.

Theories of Sport Game Aggression:

The Catharism hypothesis proposes the main function of sports today is the discharge of aggressive urges. (Lorenz, 1966, p. 271) This was thought as a symbolic substitute for war.

I think that this makes sense as this aggressive urge would explain the structure of a lot of sports that focus on aggression. Like: wrestling, boxing and the Haka in New Zealand.

However, Sipes (1973) found that sports reflect and fuel aggressive societal norms so cultures with more aggressive sports are more violent.

Furthermore, people who play combative sports are also more aggressive off the field. (Maxwell and Visek, 2009)

Black Uniforms:

Interestingly, black uniforms make players more aggressive on the field. (Frankand Gilovich, 1988)

This is because of symbolism; as black represents death and fear; as well as the referee has a bias towards teams wearing black uniforms.

The reason for these findings is because black changes how you act and are perceived by others.

In order to check this finding, the researchers used a virtual referee that watched the match with a black and white picture.

The results showed that the black uniform teams were still the most aggressive. Demonstrating how it wasn't completely the referee's bias that created these results.

Group Influence:

In their experiment, Jaffe and Yinon (1983) found when angered by a confederate; university males gave stronger shocks when in groups compared to when they were alone.

Equally, being in a group or accountable to a group can lead to a reduction in aggression as certain crimes. Like: mugging, sexual assaults and violence happen in private settings.

CHAPTER 38: CULTURAL DIMENSIONS

Cultural dimensions can be explained simply as the cultural differences in its people's values and norms.

The original theory and set of 6 dimensions were created by Hofstede and we'll look closer at his work in a moment.

But putting this into context, these dimensions can be used to explain why; for instance; British people act differently to Chinese people.

Now we can start to look at the six dimensions:

Hofstede:

In 1965, he founded the personal research department at IBM Europe, and he undertook a massive study across 40 countries.

He gave a questionnaire to over 117,000 employees which asked them about their behaviours and values.

He completed his initial study in 1973 and found six dimensions; including dimensions found after later studies.

These dimensions included: individualism versus collectivism (1980) which is where people in individualist cultures they focus on their needs and not the needs of the group. Whereas in collectivist cultures they focus on the need of the group and not themselves.

Power distance index (1980) which is the extent to less powerful members of the group except and accept inequalities. This is very closely related to how societies understand and tolerate inequalities between members. High PDI scores mean that society is tolerant of inequalities. Low scorers mean that cultures are less tolerant and require an explanation.

Critically Thinking:

As this study was done with a large sample size and it was a cross-cultural study. It gives us evidence that the study's results can be used across all cultures and that the dimensions' work for all cultures as well.

However, to improve the creditability of the study even further another research method could be used to support the findings. Such as interviews or focus groups with different cultures so their response to questions on values can be compared in more depth.

The Six Dimensions:

- Individualism versus collectivism- discussed in the case study above.

- Power Distance Index- spoken about in the study above.

- Uncertainty avoidance index- this is how tolerant a society is for ambiguity. In other words, tolerance for ambiguity means there's an openness to change as well as less strict rules.

For example, the UK is more open to change, and it has less strict rules compared to China. As they don't have freedom of speech.

- Masculinity vs. femininity- masculine societies focus on achievement, competition and wealth. Whereas feminine societies focus on cooperation, relationships and quality of life.

For example, western cultures focus on their achievement, getting the most land; a type of resource and getting the most money. Whereas, African countries; collectivist cultures; focus on the cooperation of everyone and focus on what the group needs in terms of its quality of life as well.

- Long-term vs. short-term orientation- this is the connection to the past and attitude toward the future. Short-term orientation means that traditions are kept. Long-term orientation has more of a focus on the future.

Chinese is a good example of this as they focus on their traditions. Especially in rural China whereas the UK is focusing on its uncertain future after Brexit.

- Indulgence vs. restraint- Indulgent cultures; like the western world; allow people to enjoy life and have fun. Restrained cultures; like in the east; have stricter control through strict social norms. Indulgent cultures tend to believe that they are in control of their lives; restrained cultures are more fatalistic.[1]

<u>Berry (1967)</u>

He used 120 people in each group, and he used the rice farming culture of the Temne people from Sierra Leone, the hunting, fishing Inuit people from Canada and urban and rural Scots as a reference group.

---

1 https://www.thinkib.net/psychology/page/22447/cultural-dimensions-

Additionally, each group was divided into two further groups. The people who had and the people who haven't received an education in the western world.

They brought themselves into a room and were given nine lines.

For the first two trials, they were told to match the top line as closely as they could to the other eight lines on the sheet. The instructions were given by a local interrupter in their own language. These two trials were tests to see if the instructions were understood.

For the other four trials, they were told that the other members of their culture said that a particular line was correct and then they were told to pick their own answer. For trial three the correct answer was given but for trials 4-6 the wrong answer was given. This was to test conformity.

Results showed that the collectivist culture; the Temne people; shown the highest rate of conformity and the Inuit people showed the lowest. However, within the group themselves, there was no significant difference between them for the rate of conformity. Therefore, being exposed to western culture has little difference.

Critically Thinking:

The study effectively uses several experimental groups to enable a cross-cultural comparison for their behaviour.

Although, this study lacks temporal validity; how time affects the findings; as the world has become a lot more interconnected since this study was done. So, it's very possible that the results would be different. Mainly because the Western influences are much stronger now than compared to when the study was done.

CHAPTER 39: ENCULTURATION AND ACCULTURATION

Now, I've decided to look at these two topics in the same chapter because they are very similar, and I believe that it will be easier to write and learn about them if they're in the same chapter.

Before we look at them individually both of them involve learning the cultural norms; the specific beliefs, attitudes and behaviour belonging to a specific culture.

Moving swiftly on- enculturation is the internalising of your own cultural norms from your culture of origins.

Putting this into context is that babies are not born with a culture. They learn about the cultural values and norms by learning from other people and by the process of enculturation where they learn about their origin culture and develop a cultural identity.

Demorest et al (2008):

150 trained and untrained subjects from the USA and Turkey.

Subjects listened to novel musical extracts from familiar and unfamiliar cultures. The USA, Turkey and China.

Then they completed a recognition memory task.

Results showed that subjects were significantly better at recalling music from their own culture.

But musical expertise didn't correlate with this result as Turkish subjects had expertise in American music more than their own culture because of enculturation.

In conclusion, enculturation influences memory on a deep level.

Critically Thinking:

The study has minimal if not any sample bias; when your sample is biased because you used one type of person in your sample. Like: girls, boys, British or Chinese people. This means that the findings can be applied to a wide range of people.

Although, the study was only done with two

cultures to be sure that the results can be applied to other cultures. A follow-up experiment should be done involving other cultures to show the effects of enculturation on mental processes.

Other studies:

These are some other studies that help to explain the effects of enculturation:

- Trainor et al (2012)- this study demonstrated how active learning can lead to enculturation. The example in this study was musical enculturation so learning the cultural norms of your culture's music.
- Kim and Omizo (2006)- enculturation interacts with acculturation to help create a cultural identity.
- Odden and Rochat (2004)- this study shows that active learning is not the only way how enculturation can occur. As in non-western societies, passive learning can cause enculturation as well.

Acculturation:

Now, we know what enculturation is. We now need to learn about acculturation. It's similar in a sense to enculturation because it's the internalising and learning of the norms and values of the dominant culture where you've migrated, or a more scientific definition is the psychological and cultural change that happens when a person comes into contact and interacts with a new culture.

To help us understand this concept, let's imagine that we've all moved to the USA and as we were living there and mixing with the American culture. Our behaviour would be changing because of the process of acculturation.

Furthermore, according to Berry (1997), there are four strategies that migrants can adopt to complete the process of cultural change.

These strategies are:

- Assimilation- this is where people aren't concerned about losing their connection with their origin culture, so they change their behaviour and attitudes to the norms of the dominant culture.
- Integration- people preserve their original values and beliefs but they explore relationships with other cultures as well.
- Separation- people are concerned about losing their connection to their original cultures so they actively avoid contact with other cultures.
- Marginalisation- they don't maintain their original culture and yet they don't seek contact with other cultures as well.

Dias, Da Costa and Martins (2017):

It's a correlation study so you see if there's a relationship between two things.

31,000 Portuguese subjects, 4.6% of whom were migrants.

Results showed that the prevalence of excessive weight was higher with native Portuguese than migrants.

However, the length of residence for the migrants did correlate with the prevalence of overweight.

In conclusion, the process of acculturation causes gradual changes in diets. These changes cause migrants to become more like the natives in terms of eating behaviour.

Critically Thinking:

The study used a very large sample size so it shows that the findings can be applied to culture as a whole as many people from that culture show the same behaviour

On the other hand, as it was a correlation study so a cause and effect relationship can't be established so it's unknown it this trend is caused by acculturation or another set of factors.

Other Studies:

Other studies that show the effects of acculturation are:

- Shah et al (2015)- the process of acculturation contributes to unhealthy eating behaviours due to migrants typically tend to move to a culture that promotes less healthy eating behaviours than their own culture.
- Ishizawa and Jones (2016)- there are a number of protective factors against developing obesity in migrants.

CHAPTER 40: GLOBALISATION

Personally, I do like this topic because globalisation is a pressing topic for our modern times and when learning about the topic. I knew that this process had to affect behaviour, but I didn't know how and when I learnt about it. I was interested.

However, before we learn how it affects behaviour. We must start at the beginning, or at least the beginning of the end as this is the last chapter in our social journey.

So, without further a due globalisation is the increased interconnectedness of the world.

This has happened for many reasons. Such as the internet, increased technology and more access to communication. This is because it has allowed the world to communicate more and overall helps the world to become more interconnected.

How globalisation may influence behaviour?

Globalisation can affect behaviour in several ways. Including:

The rapid increase in communication and information sharing could cause people's behaviour to become more international.

Equally, it could cause an increase in nationalism and people wanting to protect their local interests instead of global interests.

An example of the above would be the Trump Presidency as the President is focused on Make America Great Again!

Adams (2003):

Representative sample totalling 14,000 from USA and Canada.

Studied cultural values of US and Canadian Citizens in 1992, 1996 and 2000.

Results showed that cultural values didn't convergent over time. They remained very different.

For example: when the survey asked; The father of the family must be the master of his own household. The Canadian average for agreeing with the statement from 1992 to 2000 decreased from 26% to 18% whereas the American average increased from 42% to 49%

In conclusion, globalization isn't always a straightforward process in which dominant cultures subsume non-dominant cultures. The outcome of globalization depends on the acculturation strategy chosen.

<u>Critically Thinking:</u>

The study effectively shows the complexity of the process of globalisation, so it has strong internal validity.

On the other hand, this study could lack temporal validity because since 2000 the USA has grown in global power and it has grown in equal influence. So, this study should be redone to see if the results would be different and to see if the process of Americanisation (yes, it's a real word) has affected the results in these modern times.

BIBLIOGRAPHY

Lee Parker (author), Darren Seath (author) Alexey Popov (author), *Oxford IB Diploma Programme: Psychology Course Companion,* 2nd edition, OUP Oxford, 2017

Sutton, R.M., & Douglas, K.M. (2013). Social psychology. Basingstoke, UK: Palgrave MacMillan.

Alexey Popov, *IB Psychology Study Guide: Oxford IB Diploma Programme,* 2nd edition, OUP Oxford, 2018

https://www.thinkib.net/psychology/page/22447/cultural-dimensions-

Glick, P., & Fiske, S. T. (2001). Ambivalent sexism. In M. P. Zanna, (Ed.), *Advances in experimental social psychology* (Vol. 33, pp. 115-188). New York: Academic Press.

Glick, P. et al. (2000). Beyond prejudice as

simple antipathy: Hostile and benevolent sexism across cultures. *Journal of Personality and Social Psychology, 79,* 763-775.

Glick, P., Fiske, S. T., Masser, B., Manganelli, A. M., Huang, L., Castro, Y. R., et al. (2004). Bad but bold: Ambivalent attitudes toward men predict gender inequality in 16 nations. *Journal of Personality and Social Psychology, 86,* 713-728.

GET YOUR EXCLUSIVE FREE 8 BOOK PSYCHOLOGY BOXSET AND YOUR EMAIL PSYCHOLOGY COURSE HERE!

https://www.subscribepage.com/psychologyboxset

Thank you for reading.

I hoped you enjoyed it.

If you want a FREE book and keep up to date about new books and project. Then please sign up for my newsletter at www.connorwhitcley.net/

Have a great day.

CHECK OUT THE PSYCHOLOGY WORLD PODCAST FOR MORE PSYCHOLOGY INFORMATION!

AVAILABLE ON ALL MAJOR PODCAST APPS.

About the author:

Connor Whiteley is the author of over 30 books in the sci-fi fantasy, nonfiction psychology and books for writer's genre and he is a Human Branding Speaker and Consultant.

He is a passionate warhammer 40,000 reader, psychology student and author.

Who narrates his own audiobooks and he hosts The Psychology World Podcast.

All whilst studying Psychology at the University of Kent, England.

Also, he was a former Explorer Scout where he gave a speech to the Maltese President in August 2018 and he attended Prince Charles' 70th Birthday Party at Buckingham Palace in May 2018.

Plus, he is a self-confessed coffee lover!

Please follow me on:

Website: www.connorwhiteley.net

Twitter: @scifiwhiteley

Please leave on honest review as this helps with the discoverability of the book and I truly appreciate it.

Thank you for reading. I hope you've enjoyed.

All books in 'An Introductory Series':

BIOLOGICAL PSYCHOLOGY 3RD EDITION

COGNITIVE PSYCHOLOGY 2ND EDITION

SOCIAL PSYCHOLOGY- 3RD EDITION

ABNORMAL PSYCHOLOGY 3RD EDITION

PSYCHOLOGY OF RELATIONSHIPS- 3RD EDITION

DEVELOPMENTAL PSYCHOLOGY 3RD EDITION

HEALTH PSYCHOLOGY

RESEARCH IN PSYCHOLOGY

A GUIDE TO MENTAL HEALTH AND TREATMENT AROUND THE WORLD- A GLOBAL LOOK AT DEPRESSION

FORENSIC PSYCHOLOGY

CLINICAL PSYCHOLOGY

FORMULATION IN PSYCHOTHERAPY

Other books by Connor Whiteley:

THE ANGEL OF RETURN

THE ANGEL OF FREEDOM

GARRO: GALAXY'S END

GARRO: RISE OF THE ORDER

GARRO: END TIMES

GARRO: SHORT STORIES

GARRO: COLLECTION

GARRO: HERESY

GARRO: FAITHLESS

GARRO: DESTROYER OF WORLDS

GARRO: COLLECTIONS BOOK 4-6

GARRO: MISTRESS OF BLOOD

GARRO: BEACON OF HOPE

GARRO: END OF DAYS

WINTER'S COMING

WINTER'S HUNT

WINTER'S REVENGE

WINTER'S DISSENSION

Companion guides:

BIOLOGICAL PSYCHOLOGY 2ND EDITION WORKBOOK

COGNITIVE PSYCHOLOGY 2ND EDITION WORKBOOK

SOCIOCULTURAL PSYCHOLOGY 2ND EDITION WORKBOOK

ABNORMAL PSYCHOLOGY 2ND EDITION WORKBOOK

PSYCHOLOGY OF HUMAN RELATIONSHIPS 2ND EDITION WORKBOOK

HEALTH PSYCHOLOGY WORKBOOK

FORENSIC PSYCHOLOGY WORKBOOK

Audiobooks by Connor Whiteley:

BIOLOGICAL PSYCHOLOGY

COGNITIVE PSYCHOLOGY

SOCIOCULTURAL PSYCHOLOGY

ABNORMAL PSYCHOLOGY

PSYCHOLOGY OF HUMAN RELATIONSHIPS

HEALTH PSYCHOLOGY

DEVELOPMENTAL PSYCHOLOGY

RESEARCH IN PSYCHOLOGY

FORENSIC PSYCHOLOGY

GARRO: GALAXY'S END

GARRO: RISE OF THE ORDER

GARRO: SHORT STORIES

GARRO: END TIMES

GARRO: COLLECTION

GARRO: HERESY

GARRO: FAITHLESS

GARRO: DESTROYER OF WORLDS

GARRO: COLLECTION BOOKS 4-6

GARRO: COLLECTION BOOKS 1-6

Business books:

TIME MANAGEMENT: A GUIDE FOR STUDENTS AND WORKERS

LEADERSHIP: WHAT MAKES A GOOD LEADER? A GUIDE FOR STUDENTS AND WORKERS.

BUSINESS SKILLS: HOW TO SURVIVE THE BUSINESS WORLD? A GUIDE FOR STUDENTS, EMPLOYEES AND EMPLOYERS.

BUSINESS COLLECTION

GET YOUR FREE BOOK AT:
WWW.CONNORWHITELEY.NET

CPSIA information can be obtained
at www.ICGtesting.com
Printed in the USA
LVHW051321290321
682811LV00001B/6

9 781914 081415